Stardom Has Just Become More Accessible!

The
Actors Success
In The
Making

By

Christopher Healy

Acting and Understanding the Business of Show Business.

The Actors Success In The Making

Copyright

This book or portions thereof may not be reproduced or used in any form or by any electronic or mechanical means, including information storage and retrieval systems without the expressed written permission of the publisher, Studio City North, Inc except for the use of brief quotations in a book review.

Copyright © 2016 by Christopher Healy

ISBN: 978-0-9917273-5-3

All rights reserved. The information in this book is distributed on an "as is" basis, without warranty. Although every precaution has been taken in the preparation of this work, neither the author nor the publisher shall have any liability to any person or entity with respect to any loss or damage caused or alleged to be caused directly or indirectly by the information contained in this book.

Studio City North, Inc.

www.StudioCityNorth.com

Dedication

I dedicate this book to all the thousands of students I have had the pleasure and challenge of teaching, coaching and mentoring for over 25 full years. They inspired me to step up higher than I ever thought I could and offer the best of me to each of them. Bless them all.

About the Author

Christopher Healy is a family man who lives in Toronto. He has accumulated a wealth of seasoned experience, wisdom, and knowledge over 37 years in the entertainment industry, including his love of history, geopolitics, applied psychology, drama therapy and his seventeen years as a teacher, coach, and public speaker. This has shaped his unique insights, molded his passionate style and his expertise of teaching to be powerful, compelling and packed with inspiring enthusiasm!

Christopher has dedicated over 40 years of his life to the entertainment industry. Sixteen of those years was Artistic Director and Principle Acting teacher with the Toronto Academy of Acting in Toronto Canada. Christopher has been the silent achiever in nurturing the confidence, character, and creativity of thousands of kids, teenagers, and adults, including teaching his successful acting programs and youth leadership to students from all over the world. Christopher has placed dynamic "unknown" students with agencies in Vancouver, New York, Los Angeles and Toronto where many of his former students now work in TV commercials, feature films, and television. Also, he upgrades his teaching skills using the most advanced power principles of Human Needs Psychology and Strategic Intervention in learning and personal achievement; which is all used by Christopher to help give his students that successful "edge."

Christopher is author of the book titled, *"What's So Special About YOU?"* A book about learning the 77 winning qualities of the world's most successful people and applying them to change your life.

Visit: **www.ChristopherHealy.ca**

The Actors Success In The Making

Preface

I recently met one of my old students from 18 years ago. His name is Prem Singh. When I was coaching Prem, he was 16 years old. He knew nothing about the business except he wanted to be an actor. He was Canadian born and of East Indian descent. Bottom line, he was a minority and as such his reality of getting any real work was slim at best. Anyway, by his 30th birthday, he realized that no agent was going to take him. No roles were going to be giving to him. He wasn't even in the game. He had no hope. That's when he asked himself an empowering question. *"What do you have to do to become a star?"*

He realized that being a "movie star" was his only option because he was getting nothing anyway, so why not head for the top? And with that **defining life-changing thought** this young man took a filmmaking course, a scriptwriting course and more acting courses; all costing him an investment of time and money.

Then Prem went one huge step further – are you ready for this? Prem figured out that if he was going to turn his ship around from being a complete unknown and unwanted actor into a high demand "movie star" *(a goal that must seem entirely and completely insurmountable to most people, and rightly so)* he needed to learn everything about **understanding how the business of show business worked**. I mean he learnt the painstaking reality of how to create film budgets, business plans, how the financials worked with producers and with the major film / TV companies, how to negotiate and make producer deals, how to package and pitch film/TV proposals. Essentially, Prem Singh **_empowered himself_** learning everything about how movies are made from concept to screen and all the producer realities and marketing that goes along with all of that business.

Now, most people would tell you to stop right there!! But not Prem, he realized that to become a "star" you need one more magic ingredient.

The Actors Success In The Making

Prem knew that he needed to learn another massive learning task; how to become a real, viable, in-demand "BRAND."

Now, utilizing all his newly learned skills, Prem hooked up with another screenplay writer from his screenwriting class and they both created a script based upon a real East Indian boxer in Canada. Prem then pitched the story in Hollywood and got interest; he told the moneymen that he was starring in the film and he would pull in a big name to support him. The moneymen were skeptical, but they told him that if he can **surround himself with some heavyweights in the business,** then he will get his money to make his picture. Prem then went about getting top insiders to help him make the film, and he got legendary film star Mickey Rourke to co-star as his boxing coach. Bottom line, Prem created a **vortex of interest** for himself and as such he attracted all the key people from producers, stars and all the money he needed to make and promote his picture.

His film is first being released at the Toronto Film Festival 2016 and then a big splash on the movie screens.

The story about how this 16-year-old kid that I coached many years ago became a Hollywood movie star in the making (at 34 years old) is incredible, unbelievable and true. Prem sent me an email telling me all the news and also saying this *"Thank you for your coaching. I still remember your techniques, and I never forget where I come from and I would love to meet up and catch up".*

Prem also asked me to pass this message along to all my students. Read his message, and you will see it's at the core of EVERYTHING YOU NEED TO BE TO WIN! *"I just wanted to let you all know that dreams can come true, but man, you gotta work hard, learn it all, especially the business side of things, dream big and push against the Status Quo with everything you got. It's hard, but you can do it. I did it. I'm still doing it. So go and live your dreams with all your might!*

Congratulations to Prem Singh STARRING IN A HOLLYWOOD MOVIE that he co-wrote. Also co-starring legendary Mickey Rourke in the boxing movie 'Tiger'

Since my early days of teaching acting back in 1994, I use to teach and still do teach students and company's employees on *how to separate yourselves from the pack, work hard towards your dream, navigate your way through the Status Quo and play the game really, really smart.*

This concept I firmly believe in and I truly live by in my own personal career. If you are to really stand out and make an impression, you must embrace separating yourself from the pack. This is what I live by.

I am one of the few teachers in the world who has the privilege of teaching what I love and inspiring thousands of students young and old from around the world. So, when I decided to write a book about acting and how to make money in show business, I decided NOT to write about the process of "acting" because there is a ton or great books on how to be an actor. Instead, I wanted to write this book on four critically important elements that I believe will open the reader up to living their dreams for real.

Chapter One is about the business of show business. Remember, talent is what you start with, and you are going need to know the business of show business if you are going to propel yourself forward and leave the pack behind. Over the last 20 years, parents have asked me many important life and career questions about the business, and so I will answer the most important questions here in this book. In truth, you will need these questions answered to provide you some clarity, so you can make any life changing decisions based on correct knowledge.

Special Bonus Chapter Two: This bonus chapter is from my two other books *"Life Lessons From An Acting Class"* and *"What's So Special About You?"*

The information you will read is very appropriate to your learning and that's why I have included it in this book.

The excerpt from "What's So Special About You?" will offer you advice on success, performing and presentation, while *"Life Lessons From An Acting Class"* offers unique hands-on learning from the private journals of 17–21 year old students who were dedicated enough to go through my 9 week course that pushed the students beyond their perceived limits and fears, and into discovering true insights that would change their lives forever, and *can empower you to change yours.*

I have placed the bonus chapter between the chapters one and chapter three of this book because it fits there between the *understanding* and the *learning.*

I trust you will fully benefit from this bonus chapter, and it will take you to a higher level of understanding and learning, so enjoy.

Chapter Three is about what's not so readily available (except in some full time acting schools where students would pay up to $30,000 plus, but not all the schools teach this process) and that's the process of what you do when you get a screenplay or script or even a scene?

The reader may be a good actor but most actors have no real idea on how to break down that massive screenplay or script.

What I provide here for the student is a road map into screenplays, scripts and scenes and even characters, where students can learn how to navigate their way into the core of the character, picking up little gold nuggets as they go. It's important to know how to navigate your way into screenplays and pick up all the options that can help you make decisions as an actor, and then you can decide on how to play those options as *character choices*.

This is what making a good actor *great* is all about. It's about the *"playable choices"* he or she makes on screen or stage that makes an audience compelled to watch and enjoy. Acting is about making compelling choices work and these choices come from YOU making compelling decisions from all your options, which all begins when you get the script. *This chapter is GOLD!*

Chapter Four – The Winners Circle. This chapter offers you real actionable success strategies, as well as how to get yourself set-up and into the auditions circle. You will learn how to take 7 detailed steps that will take you from where you are right now and into the real auditions. At first, you won't even need an agent at least to start, but you will need to work hard, learn lots and take the 7 steps one step at a time. *This chapter takes you into acting for real!*

I also decided to approach this book as if I were your personal manager and consultant. I will provide you with insights and valuable tips to help you along the way. I will also advise you on how to develop yourself as an actor. I will also share with you how to get the agent and get the work, how to strategize your career ahead and understand the value of you as a "self-brand". Also, how to use some important promotional and marketing strategies to build your fan base!

You will learn the key insights on performing for the camera, the psychology of your character, and good screenplay essentials that every student of acting should know.

Here is the bottom line: there is more real actionable information in this book than you will find in reading twenty books on "the biz", and then trying to compile all the information together in a sequence that makes sense to you.

Add to that, thousands of dollars saved in not taking expensive courses and being scammed.

The information and strategies offered in this book have helped most of my students to find their "voice", if you will, and inspire others to hire them.

This book is about training and preparing you *for real* so get excited!

One Last Thing

If you enjoy this book or find it useful I'd truly appreciate if you'd post a short review on Amazon. Your support really does make a difference and I read all the reviews personally so I can get your feedback and make this book even better.

If you'd like to leave a review visit Amazon or Barnes & Noble or wherever you purchased this book and leave your review.

Thank you again for all your support.

Enjoy the book and thank you!

The Actors Success In The Making

Table of Contents

About the Author   iii

Preface   iv

One Last Thing   ix

CHAPTER ONE   1

I Want To Be An Actor!   1

Here Is Your Reality Check   2

How Do You Know If Your Child Or You Are Ready For A Performing Career?   4

Parents, Pressure and Child Actors   6

Separation Anxiety   6

Get The Training   7

What To Look For In A Good School Or Teacher?   9

Agents and Managers   11

What is the difference between an agent and a personal manager?   12

Contracts   12

Success In Getting An Agent   13

Do You Need To Have An Agent And A Manager?   14

What Do Agents Look At When Deciding Who To Represent As An Actor?   15

What Is An Actor's Demo Reel?   16

How Do You Choose A Good Monologue?   18

Where's A Good Place To Find A Monologue?   18

Performance Arts School Auditions   19

Giving A Professional Audition   22

What's A Good Acting Headshot?   24

When Do You Have To Join An Actor Union?   27

What Should An Actor Include On Their Resume? 28

Speaking American 30

Should I Move To LA? 31

Starting Your Business 33

Auditioning tips from Casting Director Deirdre Bowen 34

Get Started In Theater 38

Learn To Handle Rejection 38

A Good Cover Letter To Get An Agent Or Manager 40

Acting Scams 40

SPECIAL BONUS CHAPTER TWO   44

All the World's a stage 45

How do you rate with the best 50

Life Lessons from an Acting Class 52

CHAPTER THREE   68

When You Get To The "Set" 71

Set Decorum 77

Working Into The Script 80

First Reading Of The Script 85

Screenplay Format 88

Screenplay Analysis 90

Good Screenplay Essentials 90

Film Dialogue 90

Preparing To Interpret The Text 91

The Basic 6 W'S 95

C.R.O.W.S 96

Scene Analysis   97

In-Depth Scene Analysis /Character Study process   98

Why Reading Screenplays may be Difficult   101

16 Steps To Creating Your Character   101

3 Questions To Ask As Your Character   102

Super Objective, Through-Line & Obligatory Actions/Events   103

How To Choose A Super Objective   104

Motivating Desire   105

Through – Line Of Action   105

Notes On Performing For Film   107

Listening & Reading!   107

CHAPTER FOUR – THE WINNERS CIRCLE   109

Overall Success Strategies   109

10 Success Strategies For An Actor   110

7 Action steps to getting work   114

Being An Extra / Getting Experience   119

Marketing and Promotion   123

How To Use Social Media To Get More Work   124

Personal Branding   126

Here Is An Exercise For You   127

Your 10 step show business plan to acting success   130

Success Strategies For Monologues   131

Auditioning Tips   132

Tips For Comedy   134

Film, Television, Acting Definitions   134

Suggested Reading   137

The Actors Success In The Making

What's So Special About YOU?   *138*
Check Out The Classes!   *142*

CHAPTER ONE

I Want To Be An Actor!

Why do you want to be an actor? When my students tell me they want to be an actor, my first question to them is, WHY? Most times the student stares at me like a deer caught off guard, in the sudden headlight glare, of a fast moving truck.

Examine why you want to be an actor. Is it for fame and fortune? Is it to be loved by twenty million faceless strangers? Is it because it's glamorous? Is it because it looks like easy work? Is it because you want to set an example for others and change the world? Is it because you got something to prove? Is it because you want to be other characters? Is it because it's fun? Is it because you have a burning passion for Acting? Find the "why?"

If you didn't have a career as an actor, would you be acting anyway, any chance you could get regardless of pay? What would you do if you wanted to be an actor but no one will give you an acting job – now what? What other career would you have if acting wasn't an option? (Really consider this very carefully)

The actors that last to "make it" in this business are the ones who live acting to the fullest and cannot consider a life without acting worth living. It's a narrow-minded view, but they have a burning passion for acting. Watch a great film about one man's drive to be an actor in the film "Career," made in 1959, starring Tony Franciosa, Shirley MacLaine, and Dean Martin. I tell you to watch this film because this is the life you will most probably live for real. It's called survival until you make it if you ever do. After you have watched this film try asking yourself again why would you want to be an actor?

Ask yourself again and again and write down your answers. You need to reach deep into yourself and really ponder this

Chapter One

question because this decision will change your life and it may be for the better, or it may be for the worse.

Remember though, nothing in life is certain, and while only a small percentage of actors make a living acting, who says you won't be one of them? Examine why you want to be an actor.

Find the deeper purpose. This purpose needs to compel you forward through all the up's and downs until you reach your goal.

Here Is Your Reality Check

Many young people want to be actors for the wrong reasons. Usually, they want "fame" and "fortune." They think they don't need to be good in school because they are going to be a "movie star," or "top model" or a "rock star." They think this business is a glamorous business where you don't need any real experience, and you can make lots of money, have millions of strangers love you, have your photo taken by the paparazzi and best of it all, is that it requires minimal effort. It's just going to happen.

I will tell you the hard reality right here and now. Acting, singing, dancing to a professional level is tough. Trying to make a living is even tougher. In truth, working as an actor is a challenging profession at the best of times.

You need to be:

- Hungry for the roles
- Have vision
- Discipline
- Commitment
- Conviction
- Focus

The Actors Success In The Making

- Talented
- Relentless drive
- Self-confidence
- Ambition
- Passion
- Solid training
- Able to take rejection
- Be a risk taker
- Offer up a unique you
- Be marketable
- Be directable
- Be outgoing and sociable
- Carry yourself well
- Be creative
- Be self-motivated
- Be responsible
- Drive yourself hard each day and on top of all that, you need to have fun working hard and working smart.

The actor's life needs to feed your soul otherwise why would you be crazy enough to step into it in the first place?

You will be competing "tooth and nail" against other performers, all going for the same role you are. No mercy is given, and none is asked for. One performer will win, and all the rest of them will get nothing except heartbreak. Most wannabe performers are just dreamers, others are trying it for fun, while tens of millions think it's your calling; you were born to be a star!

Chapter One

In truth, most of you will give up in the first three years, and the rest of you will fall by the wayside as the years take their toll on you. Some of you will get some acting work but never enough to give up your day job or your night job. Then there will be a few of you who actually get a couple of good working years and perhaps you can buy a new car if you're lucky. A handful of you will get steady acting work for a while, and a couple of you actors may hit the "big time," whatever the "big time" means to you. Then, maybe, just maybe, one of you might become famous, a star!

How tough is it for real? Try it and find out. Either you have what it takes to compete and succeed, or you don't. No one will blow a trumpet if you enter the business, and no one will remember you when you give up years later. You still believe you got what it takes? Then welcome to show business, there is no business like it.

How Do You Know If Your Child Or You Are Ready For A Performing Career?

Let's say you have a party, or just have some work-mates over for dinner. See if your child is willing to get up and have fun performing a short commercial in front of these strangers. If your child can, then he or she will have no issues in performing for casting directors, producers, and directors.

Remember to give your child lots of time to prepare and encouragement.

When I first meet a new student, I always make an effort to shake their hand and make eye-contact with them. The reason is because I am specifically looking to see if the student will make eye contact with me or not. Will they shake my hand with a weak wrist, noodle, type of handshake or an engaged handshake.

What I am looking for are the ones who show no fear in making eye contact or shaking my hand because they have stronger self-confidence, are eager and are willing to step up and show it.

Students that don't make eye contact or offer a weak handshake are holding back and need to learn the courage to break out with their personality because personality sells!

Usually, though, my students learn to breakout and step-up to the challenges that I put to them. They know that resisting "change" is not a good thing but rather accepting change is good for them, and it's an absolute if they want to get into show business.

For more on this topic, you can follow my fulltime students who went the distance for nine weeks working fulltime with me and how they made personal journals of their experiences.

It's a wonderful learning experience about overcoming personal resistance and breaking out with your personality; the book is called "What's So Special About You?"

You can go to my site www.SpecialYouInsider.com and read up on it some more.

Chapter One

Parents, Pressure and Child Actors

This message is mainly for the Parents of newcomers to the business. Parents will often add too much pressure to the mix when their child is going for auditions. Of course, the parents want the child to do well. However, too much pressure will sap away the "fun" part of this experience. So remember, usually the first audition call is where the engagers just want to have a first look at your child to see if your child has "that something" that the casting people are looking for.

Please don't lay pressure on your child. Instead, just support and love them. Remember, you will never inspire a positive attitude in your child if, every time he or she feels that you are disappointed in them. Also, remember, not to make your child be "perfect," instead, encourage your child to be the best they can be. If your child makes a mistake, then encourage them to learn from the mistake and move on and not to give up because they made a mistake.

Children learn like sponges, and they learn from what you say and how you say it. You are a child's greatest teacher, so teach by example and don't get freaked out if they make lots of mistakes. Instead, show patients, support and try again.

Separation Anxiety

Separation anxiety, especially for infants, is a real consideration especially if you are trying to get your child into an agency. The test is simple, will your child easily go to a stranger or will he/she kick up a screaming fuss? Remember, you will be allowed to go into the casting room with your child, however when your child gets older than you are not allowed.

Anyway, your child will only have moments to get all warm and fuzzy with the casting people otherwise it's "thank you, great job, next." Please check to see if your child will need legal documents to work in the industry. For example, in the United States, a child will need a work permit from the state where he or she resides and a Social Security Card. Check with the Department of Social Services. If your child does not have this work permit, they will not be able to work on the set. So get prepared.

Other countries, please check if your child will need work permits. I am sure they will. Check with your local government.

Get The Training

If acting is something you want to try out, then I suggest schools and local theater companies. Also, you can also enhance your training with other classes at your local theater company or some schooling that can be found in your neighborhood. You should also try community theatre and look at continuing education schools. Any of these options will involve acting once a week or twice as an introduction to see if you really want to do it. All of the above provides you with an excellent understanding of objectives, intentions, the relationship with the character, finding conflict in a scene, etc. This is important when you first start working on your acting.

If you want to go professional, then there are many options for you to consider, it depends on how dedicated you are about acting and performing, how much money you have and where you live. Start by going online and start looking for professional acting schools in your area. Beware of scams. When you do an internet search of a school; search if they have a terrible reputation. If they do, you will see it in the search results.

Also, one of the most important abilities you are going to need is a vivid imagination. This is the ability to create in your head any world possible. You are also going to need to be able to read very well. Being a good reader helps you to discover new possibilities in the meaning and delivery of the words from the script. You need to learn to be able to read beneath the surface of the words and get the deeper meaning. This

Chapter One

will help stretch and develop your imagination. Training will really help you along.

You can get training for stage, theatre, improvisation, working on camera, TV commercials, how to audition, monologues, scene study, how to break a scene down, character study workshops, and work with as many teachers as you can.

Get as much experience as you can get because it's all going to help you along the way. Also, learn about the business side of show business, like, how to get an agent, about unions, about contracts, know the scams from the good agents, etc.

Example, learn from this guy: *"I have seen thousands and thousands of actors audition. And 99% of them are dull. Are unimaginative. Are the same as the last person I just saw. Because actors prepare auditions with the wrong mindset. All I know is that acting classes do not (generally) give you the skills, the techniques to 'audition.' They equip you with the skills of what to do after you have the job. It is a different skill set: to get the audition. To impress."* **Greg Apps, Casting Director Sydney, Australia.**

MY PERSONAL MANAGER TIP: Stop thinking and acting and behaving like a "bit player." Instead, truly begin thinking, behaving, feeling and acting as a "leading player"! This simple yet powerful change of "thought" alone will immediately begin to transform how you think and behave in congruence to how you want to live. The time is now to get serious and get smart, because if you don't realize that even the best runners in the world use coaches.

If you don't realize that you alone is not enough to "make it" and that your life will change immediately after you take action, then you will always do what you have always done. Is that going to be your future story? If it's time to get serious, then YOU CAN DO IT!

There are lots of work opportunities out there, and more and more people are taking smart steps to improving their own personal and performance "edge" to impress casting directors and leave their competition behind. What are you like when you go into an audition?

Do you go in just hoping to "wing-it" and hope for the best? Are you the somewhat trained, somewhat interested, somewhat of a go-getter, with a "whatever" attitude who wants to be a BIG MOVIE STAR? If you are like that, then you are living an "unfocused" dream, with no purpose and with no action to make it happen. Don't waste your life in dreams with no action.

ANOTHER PERSONAL MANAGER TIP: I encourage you to begin a visualization exercise each morning before you begin your day. I want you to visualize: ***What does success look like to you and how does it feel?*** And get excited about how it feels because if what you visualize doesn't excite you then dump it because success MUST EXCITE YOU. This is your dream of how you would live, so get excited about it.

I strongly advise you to do this exercise each day for a few minutes and help put yourself on course towards your dreams. Now, what you visualize does not have to be the same thing each day, but can be another part of what success means to you. See it for real each time you do this exercise. Just think for a moment, what would your success look and feel like to you? Get excited about it because it can become real!

What To Look For In A Good School Or Teacher?

Well, first up, how long have they been teaching? What is their learning/training background? Where have they taught before? Who have they taught? For example, I have taught thousands of students who are working in the industry, and none of them are considered "Stars" by American standards due to the fact that I teach Canadians or Europeans, and they don't have a hope of working in the US unless they have green cards. So, who the teacher has taught is not a true indicator

Chapter One

of how good they are, but it's always good to ask who they have taught that you might be familiar with.

Ask, can you contact any of their students for a reference? Ask, can you sit in on a class and see how it goes? Do they have a web/Facebook presence that you can check out?

Are they with any associations that offer "legitimacy" to their acting teaching? (Although yet again) I do not affiliate myself with any associations for two reasons.

1 / I have been an Artistic Director for 15 years with the Toronto Academy of Acting which is a reputable and high profile school.

2 / I have discovered even in my own research that even these "associations" that claim to offer teacher "credibility" are so often full of "club politics" and discriminations that I will not associate myself with any of them that claim to offer me "legitimacy."

And in truth, I was an Artistic Director years before most of these "associations' ever became legitimate themselves, so no thank you!

Perhaps you are already an actor, and then I would suggest getting out into the reality of the auditions. Here you get to test your skills for real against other actors. Here in the audition arena, you will learn what works in the audition. Being an actor is great, but if you are lousy at auditions, you will not be a working actor.

Also, you should take classes from as many teachers are you can because, in truth, you always learn from every teacher. What you put into it, is what you get out of it. Even the best in the world needs to continue training and keep their skills sharp.

All up, you want to know about the teachers or schools experience, their background. Sit in on a class and talk to some of their previous students, and you will get a better idea of the person and or the school and then make your decision accordingly.

Agents and Managers

In the United States, agents receive, by law, ten percent. In Canada and most other western countries, agents receive anywhere from 10% to 25% depending on what the job is that you did. Also, how well the agent is doing in business and how the government does or does not regulate agent's fees is another factor as to why some agents may charge more fees. Managers usually get fifteen percent but can be higher.

A manager's job is to give you a career direction in the industry. The manager should look at you through the lens of the bigger picture, your possible career, and not just an acting job. This is what I do when I am looking at one of my students; I try to see them down the road within the bigger picture. Is that student more than just one or two acting jobs? Do they have the potential to work across the mediums of TV commercials, Television, Film, Stage and even voiceovers? Do they have the hunger, passion, commitment and drive to navigate themselves along? Do they have what it takes to learn the networking savvy? These are important considerations when I choose a student to be recommended for a top class agent and access to real acting work. Managers should look at your real potential as a viable commodity in the market; however, most agents don't do that because most of the talent they represent don't have that "big picture" career potential. They just have a very limited lifespan.

Managers are supposed to guide you with things such as your photos, how your resume should look, and how to get work.

Also, if they are good, they will talk to you about how you get from where you are today, to where you want to be in say, five years. Managers work out a plan of action that the both of you will work through to get you to your goals. They may also work out ways to get you noticed by certain people like directors or producers. For example, I have taken under my wing to manage about fifteen students in as many years, and I develop them and educate their parents for the industry. I lay out the future plans for the student and let them know that I am essentially a "bridge" between where they are now, and where they need to be. I guide them through the jungle of confusion and scams, to a more reputable agent or manager and then they are off and running.

What Is The Difference Between An Agent And A Personal Manager?

In the US, the agent will negotiate the job on your behalf. Casting directors will call the agent with a call-time for an actor to audition. The agent then calls the actors manager and passes the information onto the manager. The manager then calls the actor and gives them the call time. That's how the American system works, but in Canada, the agent gets the call from the casting director, and then the agent calls the actor directly.

If you book the acting job, your agent negotiates with the producers of the show, your pay, which would be based on if you are a union actor, or non union (more on this a little later). If the role is a big part, the manager will probably jump in and help you all they can. But the first rule is this: rely on yourself.

Contracts

I can't give you much advice here because there are many contracts with their own wording. However, in regards to agents and their contracts; make sure that you know how many years the contract binds you up for. My advice is try to get one year with the agent to see how it goes, and then after the first year, you can sign a new contract for a longer term. Before you sign a contract, review it thoroughly; make sure you understand what it is saying. Get professional help if needed but make sure you know what you are signing. Look for the "out" clause, just in case that they don't get you an audition within say six months. If they don't get you out to a reasonable amount of auditions over a six month period, then you may want to consider leaving them with a written letter.

A reasonable amount of time needs to be worked out by you and the agent or manager, but how about say, two auditions a month? IF you don't get a minimum of two auditions a month, then talk to your agent or manager and see what could be holding you back. Are your photos doing the job of effective representation? What about your audition technique? Are your skills up to par as in a completive level? Don't automatically blame the agent. Lots of factors play into why you're not getting auditions so talk to your agent.

Next, I would look to see if the industry its self is slow. That happens in a sluggish economy. If all were okay, then I would seriously consider leaving the agent or manager, but do it in a professional and respectful manner.

How do I do that? You first sit down with your agent and express your concerns in the matter and get their feedback, perhaps they really want you to stay and would like to try and work things out.

On the other hand, maybe they too will see that the relationship is not working, and they agree with you that you should leave. Then you would notify them in writing of your intent to end the relationship/agreement, and that would be at the end of 14 days. Then go in and pick up any photos or resumes or demo reels that you left with them, and thank them for their time and effort and you leave on good terms.

Success In Getting An Agent

I believe that you should rack up as much experience in non union work before going to get an agent. Both you and the agent benefits very nicely if you have experience. Having said that, it's extremely valuable to have an agent as they can get you to auditions that can lead you to paid work in television, film, theater and even voiceovers. If you are doing a stage show, then your objective is to get the agent to come and see your show. This is essential since many agents won't consider representing an actor until they've seen them on stage, TV, film or the actor performs a monologue or presents a demo reel.

Actors that have the most success in getting an agent are those who actively call agents and invite them to their upcoming shows. Don't assume that just one contact will be enough; remember the agents are very busy people. Keep the agents informed about your projects by sending them any new works, updates in emails, or in promotional postcards, and continue to invite them to the shows you appear in. So, get into as many non union shows as you can – no excuses! Put together a list of agents, managers, and casting directors so you can send them your headshot and invite them to your shows.

Remember, when you are mailing a package to an agent or manager, you need to have a great actor's headshot, a cover letter, and a resume. Remember, if you have talent and don't give up, then it is possible that you will get one agent to say yes! And then you are on your way to becoming an actor.

Do You Need To Have Both An Agent And A Manager?

No, you don't. However, it's easier to find an agent with a manager in the US than it is in Canada. In Canada, you will find some principle agents who are also managers.

Those agent/managers are top of the line. Other lower level agents in Canada sometimes "tag" the "personal manager" label onto their agent name but it's only a tag. You can find an agent on your own if you have the determination and you know what you are doing.

In the US I would try to get a manager first, and they will get you the agent but in Canada go for the agent.

What Do Agents Look At When Deciding Who To Represent As An Actor?

Agents and managers, casting directors, producers, and directors will look for most of the following. They look into your eyes searching for your passion, your energy, and that winning personality. Remember, personality always did sell, always does sell and always will sell. They look at your talent on any videos, or showreels, your honesty in performance, do you keep things simple or do you over complicate a performance? They look at your training, your experience, your "type of look." For example, are you a light-hearted look, commercial look or dramatic look?

They look at your body; do you look like a paratrooper or a wimp? Do you have a sexy look or a plain Jane look? "Plan Jane" look could be exactly what they are looking for, so don't put yourself down if you don't look like a top model. If you are a child, then look happy and be energized with a bright personality. Casting people look at everything they can and go with their gut reaction. Welcome to show business. First impressions are all important in this game. They will also look at your abilities, do you sing, dance, play a musical instrument, is your voice good for voiceovers, are you easy to talk to, your availability and your commitment.

In theory, it would be great if you were the only person an agent represents (that fits your profile), so you would have a greater chance to win roles. In reality, the agent has two, perhaps three others that look just like your type, and then there are all the other agents with their own list of actors to show the casting director. So "competition" is the name of the game, get used to it.

Remember, when you are being interviewed by an agent, you are also interviewing them. So, smile, ask relevant questions like: how many people do you have on your books? What are your commissions? How long is your contract good for? Is there an "out" clause in your contact if the relationship is not working between us? How long have you been an agent? Ask questions and see if you like the agent. Do you get a good vibe? An ideal "win-win" situation would be if the chemistry and respect between you and the agent/manager were amazing! That's what works well.

What Is An Actor's, Demo Reel?

A demo reel is a promotional marketing tool that shows scenes from your projects that you have done. Usually, the reel will have three different scenes and varied looks. The demo tape or showreel will usually be about 3 to 5 minutes long and be of professional-looking footage, sound, and quality. If the demo reel looks like crap and sounds like crap then trash it because that's exactly what the agent or manager or producer will do. You need to put your best foot forward to make a professional impression. You don't put your dirty crappy shoe forward, NEVER.

Remember, when you complete an acting job, always ask the producers if you can have a copy of your work for inclusion into your demo reel. Sometimes you have got to be persistent in trying to get a copy of your work, so get a copy. When you have your copies of at least three scenes, you then take the tapes to an editing production house (Google "editing production"), and they will review all your work, and work out the best way to piece the best bits together. They will also want your name for the reel and any other information like your agent or managers contact info.

If you don't have them, then put your own contact info on it. Be advised; editing is a very time laboring process and the editor is going to charge you hundreds of dollars. In fact, you can pay as must as $600 per day in an editing booth, so, make sure you get the cost in advance before they begin the work.

Is a demo reel really important? YES! Go to YouTube and view actors reels.

MY PERSONAL MANAGER TIP: If you don't have scenes to use then make a demo yourself. Pick two contrasting scenes and have it shot in movie quality with excellent sound and picture quality, no longer than 3 minutes in total. The idea is: If I were to look at your reel then I would "think" feature film. Also, when you have your name appear at the start of your demo reel, make sure it appears the way it would appear if it were an actual movie. For example, start with a black screen, and then your name fades up in white on the black background.

Remember, you're not trying to fool anyone, but you are trying to present the "idea" of you being "feature film" potential. Don't try to mislead them into thinking you did those movies. Just start with your name fading in on black, and then fade away. Then your first scene "title name" appears on black and then fades into that scene.

Remember to make this first scene your best, and then a crossfade to black for a moment, and then into the name of the next scene, and then go into that scene. If you are adding music, do NOT add a song that is world famous to you name appearing. Keep it simple. You do not want them thinking you're "breaking copyright."

Also, when adding music to a part of your scene, try using "stringed instruments" because that's what they use in films. Again, do not over do it. Once the last scene is finished, you then repeat your name one last time as you did at the start, and then add your contact information as in phone, website OR agent contact if you have an agent. Get them to go to your website by adding, "For more, visit me at www....."

Chapter One

How Do You Choose A Good Monologue?

Well, first up, a well-trained actor is always prepared with at least three monologues, a modern (contemporary) comedy, a dramatic piece, and a William Shakespeare piece. In your case, have a comedy (lighthearted) and a dramatic (heartfelt) monologue ready to perform.

Keep the performance simple and keep it real. Choose a monologue that you like, a monologue that moves your spirit speaks to your heart. Try to make it your age and gender, male or female. You will need to read a lot to find something you like. Try to do a monologue no longer than 1 ½ minutes in length. If it is longer, then edit out some of the lines and keep all the key information that moves the story along to its natural end.

Make sure you are able to perform your monologues both for the camera and for the stage – yes there is a big difference, and you had better know how to perform those differences.

Where's A Good Place To Find A Monologue?

Go to the Internet and type in "monologues." You can also look for monologues in bookstores. Some students have asked me over the years if I thought it was a good idea to write their own monologue. My answer to that is not really. First, understand that a monologue is a structured piece of writing and writing a monologue is a craft, it's a learned skill to write well. My advice is to let the professional writers write the monologues, and you bring them to life. If you have to write something for yourself, then write from what you know.

MY PERSONAL MANAGER TIP: When auditioning with monologues: Children 8 years old and under, prepare only ONE monologue (approx. 45 seconds): no stage scripts, no songs, no rhyme, no accents, no speeches. Do not write or have someone write a monologue for you. You should not have profanities unless swearing is crucial to the storyline and at the heart of your character. You must be 100% memorized. You want to "feel" the part rather than "act" the part. "Acting" is pretending unless you feel something for the character and for the words, you are speaking as the character.

When auditioning with a monologue, do not use props unless critical to your performance. If your monologue is from a movie, do not make the mistake of "duplicating" what you saw.

They don't want to see you be Brad Pitt, instead, make it your own version by bringing something unique or special from you to the scene. Be prepared to deliver the monologue sitting or standing, stage or screen.

When going to perform your monologue, make sure you wear comfortable clothes. Do not wear hats because they cover your hair, and cast a shadow across your eyes. When performing, do not wander around the floor aimlessly. Only move when you have the characters 'impulse" to move. Make your moves clear with clarity and motivation. If you sit, know why you sit. If you stand, know why you stand. If you cry, don't fake it but cry for real. If you laugh, laugh for real, and don't fake it, and know what's making you laugh.

Keep your performance honest. Don't try to look older than your age. Use minimal makeup and have your hair clean and out of your face. Bring your headshot, resume and demo reel if you have one.

Performance Arts School Auditions

The information below is what I supply my students doing a performing Arts school audition. So, use this how you will and apply to your personal situation.

Remember it's not about learning words, it's about walking up on stage in front of strangers who will be judging their every moment, word, pause, every step, every hand gesture,

Chapter One

every tone inflection, and ultimately giving the performance of their life. Otherwise, that student won't get into the school of their choice. And if that's not a real issue then okay, do an hour of quick preparation and hope for the best. Otherwise all I am saying is be prepared to go extra time if needed. I always tell my clients: **Proper Planning Prevents Poor Performance.**

Last year I worked with five girls to get into performance schools, and all five got in. However, the work to get them ready was hard as we went through the monologue word by word, line by line and thought by thought just to start.

I normally then record the student's monologue and that way we can see what improvements need to be made, and then we reshoot again and again and again making little improvements as we go, as well as the student, is feeling more confident.

I have also attached here a **video of training** (https://youtu.be/bcZGVK_g-CY) that a student should use to help their audition performance. When looking at the video just follow the instructions line by line through the monologue. Simply go through each line of the monologue working through it as the video says.

A monologue is an uninterrupted speech by a character. The character may be speaking his or her thoughts aloud, directly to another character, or speaking to the audience.

Below are some guidelines for you to keep in mind when doing an audition performance on stage.

The Actors Success In The Making

Evaluation:	4	3	2	1
Preparedness	Student is completely prepared and has obviously rehearsed.	Student seems pretty prepared but might have needed a couple more rehearsals.	The student is somewhat prepared, but it is clear that rehearsal was lacking.	Student does not seem at all prepared to present.
Enthusiasm	Facial expressions and body language generate a strong interest and enthusiasm about the topic in others.	Facial expressions and body language sometimes generate a strong interest and enthusiasm about the topic in others.	Facial expressions and body language are used to try to generate enthusiasm, but seem somewhat faked.	Very little use of facial expressions or body language. Did not generate much interest in topic being presented.
Posture and Eye Contact	Stands up straight, looks relaxed and confident. Establishes eye contact with everyone in the room during the presentation.	Stands up straight and establishes eye contact with everyone in the room during the presentation.	Sometimes stands up straight and establishes eye contact.	Slouches and/or does not look at people during the presentation.
Pitch	Pitch was often used and it conveyed emotions appropriately.	Pitch was often used but the emotion it conveyed sometimes did not fit the content.	Pitch was rarely used OR the emotion it conveyed often did not fit the content.	Pitch was not used to convey emotion.
Memorization	100 % Memorized	75% Memorized	50% Memorized	25% Memorized

Chapter One

Giving A Professional Audition

When you arrive at the audition (on time) greet the auditors and offer your headshot and resume. Fill out any paperwork and take a look at any additional information like storyboard shots for you to get familiar with what's required. They may ask you your name and what you will be performing. If you have some time, find a place to relax and breathe. Just keep taking long, slow deep breaths.

FORGETTING YOU LINES

Forgetting your lines is every actor's nightmare, and it happens to everybody at some point or another. So if you do forget a line, don't panic, stay in character, remember to breathe and simply repeat the last line you just said, and this will most likely jog back your memory. If you have to, then improvise a few lines until you get back on track. Remember, the auditors are looking at you as an actor, so keep composure and your confidence no matter what.

MOVEMENT

Lots of actors make the mistake of staying rooted to the floor during their audition. This tactic can be boring to watch. Instead, play around the stage area believably; meaning know your monologue well enough to 'feel" the impulse to move. Remember this audition is like a mini-play, so bring what you need to make it all work.

STANDING ON STAGE

Place yourself about 10 feet away (or as the space of the room permits). If you're on a stage, don't hide yourself so far upstage that they can't see you that well. Don't play your scene to the judges or auditors. Pick an imaginary character that you're character would be talking to, and place that imaginary character close to the judges.

Don't directly take to the auditors in your monologue. They want the freedom to sit back and enjoy your performance and not be a part of it. Also, don't look at the audience but stay connected to the imaginary person in front of you that you are meant to be talking too.

WHEN IT'S OVER

When you finish your last line, hold them moment for a few seconds and then look up to the judges with a smile and say "thank you." They may say thank you in return, and then that's it. Turn and walk off. Do not linger around and do not ask questions. However, if you are asked a few questions, then be friendly and have a pleasant conversation. Do not talk and talk and talk. Make your answers brief and to the point.

So, when you are rehearsing, make sure that you have thought about some of the questions that may ask you and have a few ready answers.

If you can get a coach, I would strongly advise you to get coaching. Just because you know the lines, and know your character's objective, does not mean you have a wonderful performance. In truth, your performance will probably still be "okay." A good coach can and will see all the problems you can't. They look at the performers 'bigger picture. They are trained to examine issues and know how to help you take your performance to a professional level. Do yourself a big service and GET COACHING!

Lastly, don't walk into the audition with low energy. Bring your positive energy and interest to what's happening. Be genuine and pleasant. Speak clearly. Make eye contact. Listen to what's being said. Ask questions. Showcase your upbeat personality and attitude together with some spontaneity. Do not be shy, or have low energy or a crappy attitude.

Finally, remember to have fun and don't be late.

Chapter One

WHAT'S A GOOD ACTING HEADSHOT?

(Photo of William Healy)

A good acting headshot is simple and focused. The eyes reveal the presence of who you are in a moment. It's that simple and yet to get that simplicity takes an excellent photographer, who is good at getting the actor to relax, and show their personality.

The photo should look like you on a good day and NOT a passport photo. A successful photo reflects what you look for in an actor – *a compelling personality*, someone you want to meet face-to-face. The photo should enhance, not mislead. Relax, enjoy and appreciate yourself, and you will get a good headshot. Be sure to get your picture updated every few years.

MY PERSONAL MANAGER TIP: When you are having your photo done, just before the shot is taken, you want to be thinking a powerful thought (use your imagination here) that nobody needs to know about except you.

And you keep that thought while the photos are being taken. You can have a fun thought or a happy thought, whatever brings out your personality.

What this does is put an emotionally powerful thought behind the eyes that really gets you fired up. That emotional fire will be in your mind and can be seen in the eyes on the photo. The idea is that you want the person looking at your photo to see "something" in your eyes, and so you should make that "something" as special as possible or as fun as possible.

ANOTHER PERSONAL MANAGER TIP: Remember to make sure that your photo is printed on semi-gloss or low sheen paper and NOT full gloss. The reason for this is that when you hold the photo up, the light glares across the full gloss, making it hard to read your name – this is a no, no.

To find an excellent photographer you want to look at their work and see their style. My personal experience of working with acclaimed photographer Helen Tansey is amazing. Check out her website at http://sundariphotography.com.

Also, go online and look for headshot photographers, look in the trade papers. Expect to pay anywhere from $250 - 500 dollars for a photo session and ask, does that include a make-up artist?

Here are some other questions to ask: What exactly do I get for my money? How many rolls of film do they use up in the session? How many "looks" should I go for? (I suggest three, a natural look, a commercial look, and a character look).

Chapter One

The Natural look is you looking fresh, clean and happy. Wearing natural clothes that best enhances your style of feeling relaxed.

Don't look overly prepared for the photo, like, try not to wear too much make-up. The commercial is vibrant. Try looking at the latest fashion magazines and look at the ads pages to get a better idea of the commercial look. The last look is the character look. To get this look, try being a character. Create a character. You might even suggest the photographer to use dramatic lighting if your character is dramatic. Also, ask, do I get a proof sheet? How many 8 x 10's do I get with that cost?

What is the cost of getting reprints done? What type of clothing should I bring to the session?

You want to meet with the photographer, see their work and talk to them. Get a feel of their personality; can you work with this person? Do you feel comfortable with them? If you don't feel comfortable then simply let them know that you will think about it and leave. After you have given it some real thought, if you still feel uncomfortable, then don't go with them. Look at other photographers until you feel you have found the right one for you.

You can also check with American SAG – Screen Actors Guild website, and ask about reputable photographers. In Canada, click onto the ACTRA website and do the same with them. In other countries, you can look up your national Acting or Theatre unions, and ask them for reputable photographers that they may know of.

Let them know what you want, and ask if they know of any good photographers. You can also ask them about reputable agents.

When Do You Have To Join An Actor Union?

The union situation in the United States is different than Canada and the UK, and you should check out the American SAG – Screen Actors Guild. In Canada, check out ACTRA, and the British Actor's Equity website for updated information about joining unions.

First of all, what is a "union"? The unions make sure that the actors are treated well and fairly. They make sure you are not overworked, that you get paid for your work, or if you work overtime, you will get paid that extra money. They make sure that you get proper rest periods and full lunch periods, and that's just the basics of how unions protect you. If you are "non" union, then you may still be treated fairly, for example, get proper rest periods, and full lunches, but you won't get as much money as a "union" actors. This is not a bad thing when you first are starting out because what the non union productions really offer you is on the job experience and plenty of it.

That said, you start off as a NON union actor and build your experience until you are offered a UNION job. Once you get that job that's an "acting credit' or what they call "permit" for that job, you then pay the union for that credit, and then you do the job. Don't be in a hurry to get into the union to early. Remember, you are going to need experience first, and you can get that experience in the NON union work that's out there. Once you become union you will not be able to go back and do NON union work; so make sure you get your experience in non union first and then move up into the union.

MY PERSONAL MANAGER TIP: Make sure you don't rush into a union to early, because in the auditions you will be competing against experienced union actors and you will be overlooked due to your inexperience.

The solution to this is to get lots of non union experience before you become union.

What Should An Actor Include On Their Resume?

Google "sample actors resume," and you will see lots of examples. On the resume, your name goes at the top, on the left side eye color, hair color, weight, any unions.

Place your strongest experience first; for example, say you have lots of TV commercial experience then put that first. If you have movies or theatre - whatever is your strongest, will go first. Next, place second you're not so strongest and so on. Also, include dance or any singing you may have taken.

Remember, if you can sing, dance and play a musical instrument as well, you increase the chances of getting acting work, as opposed to an actor who can only act.

Last on your resume are special skills, like can you ride a horse or drive a car? If your line of credits gets too long for the page, you remove the least impressive work and replace that with good work credits.

Just remember your most significant credits always go to the top.

See next page for a sample resume template

NAME
Non Union

Height: 5' (152cm)
Weight: 94lbs
Age: 15
Eyes: Dark Brown
Hair: Dark Brown

Home address
Phone
Email

EXPERIENCE: FILM / TV / STAGE

Name of show	Role	Production	Director
Ghosts in Sight	Tina (Lead)	West side productions	Jon Smith

TRAINING

PUT WHAT YOU'RE STRONGEST IN FIRST.
Example:

Graduated Christopher Healy's (SCNTV) Actors Intensive Training courses
- Improvisation, movement and character discovery using Meisner Technique
- TV commercials (also working with products)
- How to Audition for TV commercials and feature films
- Acting for the camera intermediate – advanced / working on multiple scenes on camera
- Working in an "on set" environment, learning techniques, terminologies and process

ANY DANCE / SINGING TRAINING OR OTHER TRAINING GOES IN HERE.

Example: Two years of Jazz classes and two years of Musical Theatre at Name of studios

INTERESTS / HOBBIES

Acting, Directing, Designing, Writing,

SPECIAL SKILLS

Piano, Dance, Basketball, Biking, Long boarding,

MY PERSONAL MANAGER TIP: Use plain standard white paper and nothing fancy, also use simple to read font and again nothing fancy or cute. Remember to keep your resume "professional" and updated.

Chapter One

Speaking American

When it comes to accents, I always tell my students that the best accent they should work on first is the "American non-regional accent" or speaking American without an accent. The reason for this is that most productions in North America are made in the United States. If you want to work in the movies or on television, then I would suggest that you work on having an American non-regional accent. This accent sounds American, but you can't tell from where in the United States they come from, they just sound American.

Even in Canada, they produce most shows with Canadians that sound "American" because the producers want to sell their shows to a much more lucrative American market and not just to a small Canadian market.

Now, there are different sets of audio disks that are considered good introductions to different dialects. Google: David Alan Stern and try Jerry Blount, also Jillian Lane-Plescia.

Also, Google "American non-regional Accents".

MY PERSONAL MANAGER TIP: Try listening to a recording of your voice, and you will hear how different you sound from what you think you sound like. When you speak, you actually hear the vibration, resonance of your own voice through your bones and muscles in your face. However, when you hear your voice from a recording, you are actually hearing it how others hear it. So, practice your accent using a recording device, and you will get faster results. Finally, if you can afford it, try working with a good dialect coach. They can really teach you dialects so that you will sound like the real thing. Google "Dialect Coaches."

Should I Move To LA?

Is it necessary to move to L.A. or New York to begin an acting career? That's a big question with profound implications for YOU! So, let's take into serious consideration the following.

First up, are you of legal age to make such a move? Truth is, many young girls and boys want to be "movie stars" and run away from home to Hollywood or to New York to make the "big time." In reality, within a few weeks, they find themselves surviving on the streets where they become beacons for predators. Welcome to the jungle!

Predators are men or women who will tell you what you want to hear just to get you to trust them. They may even give you food and money and a place to stay, but it's going to cost you big time sooner or later. In truth, many (not all) of the kids that find themselves in this situation usually end up as sex slaves in prostitution houses, or they end up in the dark pornographic world of child sex films, or they end up dead somewhere. If that scares you, good! It's a horrifying reality that you face if you are underage and run away to the "big time." Oh, that won't happen to me you might say. Really? Are you feeling lucky enough to put your life on the line?

MY PERSONAL MANAGER TIP: If you are a young kid, stay home and get into theatre or start a theatre troupe. Get other kids that love acting and put on plays, make movies and develop yourself slowly. Do great in school; learn all you can because I am here to tell you, that you are going to need an education. If you are a poor reader or writer, then get GREAT at reading and writing. Use your time wisely to get training. Do plays in Community Theater, read up on your craft and on some of your favorite Hollywood stars and see how they did it. If you live in Canada or another country and you are serious about trying your luck in the US, then you had better see about getting a work permit or a green card.

Google: "Green Card," "American work permits," "can foreign actors work in America." Do your research here on the

Chapter One

realities. If you are already an America, then the question for you is shall I move to New York or LA? Do your research and training and when you are old enough then consider the following. Do you feel good enough to go the distance of living in either New York or Los Angeles?

Remember, you will need to have financial support to make that move. You will need money for rent, food, living expenses, and travel expenses just to start with.

Also, consider this: have you taken acting classes? Have you got any acting experience so far in the theatre or film or TV? Do you have good newspaper reviews of your shows? Do you have a demo reel ready as a marketing tool? Have you got photos ready to go? How are you going to live day to day? Are you going to wait on tables or create a company that can support you while get going? Are you going to work in a store? What are you going to do to live and survive while living your dream? Have you done your reconnaissance homework on where are the agents located? Where are the production houses? Find out where the productions are and where the work is.

Have you checked the trade papers to see what the work situation is? Is work in those cities slowing down due to the weak economy? Have you looked at production work in South Carolina, Chicago or in Toronto Canada or Vancouver?

Lots to consider so take your time and plan your moves in advance and then develop yourself to those goals. Finally, if you are not an American, then you are going to need something called a "Green Card" to legally work in the United States. Google: How to get an American Green Card and find out. Good luck!

Starting Your Business

Alright, you have the dream, so now let's see what you will need to make it into a real business. You will need the "business plan." Your business plan is the most important first thing you will need because this will outline in detail your short-term goals that will lead to your long-term goals, and ultimately, your vision of success. The business plan is your realistic roadmap to success. If you don't plan for your success, then, as they say, you plan for failure.

Start your business plan with your vision, your dream and write it down in one clear and precise sentence – what is your dream? What does success look like to you? Write it out in detail, so if I were to read what success looks like to you, it would excite me because it excites you. So get excited about what you write!!

Next, you will need finance (money). Get your parents to invest in your potential and your dream. Use that money to get training and then more training, get photos, resumes, cover letters, envelopes, stamps, marketing materials, fax, phone, and any office expenses. Once you have those short-term goals set up, your next goal will be to get out and get non-union work.

Get as much NON union acting work to build up your acting experience for your resume, and perhaps a demo reel.

Also, try to get as much extra work as possible for the experience. Give yourself at least two years in the field getting as much non union acting work as possible. Just get out there and rack up the experience.

Next, figure out what your "type" is, and what I mean is, are you a tough guy or perhaps a nerd? Maybe you're a business person? You need to see what your "type" is to understand better how an agent might market you. Also, what type of auditions you might go to. Try asking some friends and family what they think your type is. Find out how people see

Chapter One

you, and if that lines up with how you see yourself, then you can market yourself accordingly. Also, take into consideration your look in each medium. For example, some people look better on the small screen while others look better on the big screen. How about you?

Auditioning tips from Casting Director Deirdre Bowen

Casting Director, Deirdre Bowen is President of the Casting Directors Society of Canada. She took some time to explain the auditioning process to Branch Line editor, Jackie Laidlaw. Deirdre started her career in 1974 as casting assistant at CBC and worked her way up to become a casting director at "the Corp." In 1980 she moved on to become an independent casting director in film and television, where she sits as one the most respected in the business.

What is the biggest mistake made in an audition?

Two things, the BIGGEST is lack of preparation. Be on top of your material. Learn the lines! This is not a memory test. Give the part – even if it is a few lines – a beginning, middle, and end. Think the part through creating the scene, place yourself. The second would be trying to make the part bigger than it is. Throw it away! Casual, naturalistic reading, please! It is not what's on the outside, but the inside. This should be the easiest thing to do, but we all know that nerves and desire for the part come into play. So be prepared, and be natural.

How do you decide who gets the audition?

It all has to do with the material. My job is to match the person with the script. I bring in four people per role. One would be the image dictated by the script. Then I find different ways for the part to go. Casting directors do have lists. We bring in the first few people on our lists. We bring in the first few people on our listings that qualify for the part. It is not a matter of playing favorites. Some directors

34

have their favorites, and that is boring for the casting director.

If actors are not getting auditions what do you suggest they do?

I don't give first-time opportunities to actors. Other casting directors do. Sometimes we take a chance on a new actor, but mostly I am looking for people who have a resume we can build on. (There) Was a time we could see everyone eventually. The business is so big now; there are so many actors out there. But if you're not getting the auditions you want, maybe you don't have the talent for that big of a part. Look more clearly at what you are doing, and how you are doing it. Perhaps your strength is different that the way you perceive yourself. Sometimes, it is a matter of reassessing your technique going back to class, or being more prepared for the audition. Every actor has an opinion of their talents. Some see themselves as leading characters, when they will always be seen for smaller parts, but could make a good living at it. I have opinions about actors' talents most people have varying degrees of talent that can be utilized.

How should actors who aren't known by you get your attention? And, how do you feel about actors contacting you?

Get a good agent. Look seriously at what parts are out there for you – talk to your agent. If you get a good part, let me know. Send me a fax, or a postcard and describe the part. I read them.

How do I feel about actors calling me?

I don't take the calls. That's why I have an assistant. What can I do? Some actors I loathe to bring in, if they were crazy to me on the phone. How will I be sure they won't be the same in the audition? I don't mind if their agent is ringing me up to find out why their actor didn't get the audition. Often the answer is that performer qualifies for the audition, but didn't make the shortlist cut.

Chapter One

What are the reasons for not getting the part?

Sometimes, but not often, it is from a really rotten audition. Usually, it is because the project went in a different direction. Or physically they needed a contrasting look to another character. Or the part got written out.

Should actors dress for the part?

Yes, to give the impression, but don't go overboard. If it is a cop, wear a crisp shirt, because the character is crisp. Don't take away from the performance though. If the character is a slob, don't be such a slob that they are looking at your clothes.

How important is a resume to you and the director?

Directors don't pay attention to your resume. We do. Casting directors look for both your credits and your schooling. Also to see who you have worked with.

How important is the relationship between the director and the actor?

The audition is your rehearsal. Especially in television, the one-on-one time with the director is at the audition. There is no time on set, or before.

What is really said when we leave the room?

Sometimes nothing. Production matters or what we're eating for dinner. I suggest the director write notes to himself. And if it so on tape, I insist that the director go back and look at the tape, because people get missed.

What is involved with being a casting director?

My first priority is to the production, not the actors. I try to secure the best person, for the best price, matching the right person with the script. There is a lot of organizational stuff and paperwork. We are the producers' representatives, negotiating the contracts with the agent. It is difficult to do well, much like acting because there is no clear definition of what is a good casting director. But I have to go out and get the jobs too, from the production companies.

Chapter One

Get Started In Theater

The theater is a great place to begin your career, even if its community theater, just get involved and have fun. Try seeing plays, comedy, drama, musicals, large productions or a one-person show, just go and learn and enjoy. Remember, the people on that stage are living their dream. Watch them and learn. When you do theater, you have to learn about your character, learn lines, create and work with others, and step out on stage opening night to feel the exhilaration

Do yourself a favor and try theater, it's a magical experience. Do one play after the next and build your experience, build your resume, build your potential, build your confidence, build your network of friends, build your career from the ground up. Audition for everything and learn from each audition experience. Volunteer for productions, just get active, get involved and get to making it happen. Check local papers or local internet sites for theater productions going on in your community.

Learn To Handle Rejection

This is a big one - When you put yourself out there as a performer, you will face rejection at some point, especially in the auditions. The truth is, you must not let it get to you on a deeply personal level. Try and try again, don't quit, but rather learn from each audition experience and get better at it, and then you will see, someone will say YES!

As an example, my son Nicholas was with an agent for a year, and during that time he did about 25 auditions, had six callbacks but no "yes." Now think about it for a moment, that's 25 rejections over a year for an eight-year-old boy, and on the 26th audition, they said YES!

The Actors Success In The Making

The photo below is of Nicholas Healy (which is full of personality) for a Canadian Tire commercial. Please note: This photo is NOT for an actor's regular headshot, but it is full of personality, to say the least.

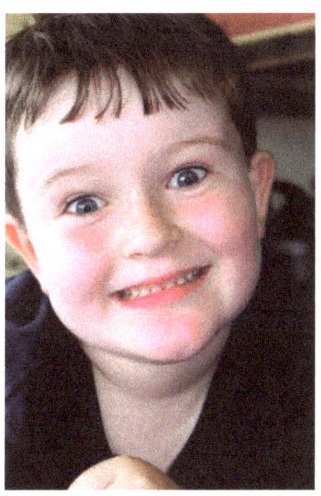

My other son, William, he went into the business and received his first "YES" on his fourth audition, and was in an episode of Warehouse 13.

Then he had around 30 more auditions with about 20 callbacks and got nothing. This is the business. You keep going forward, and improving, and taking classes, and improving, and marketing, and improving, and auditioning until they say *"YES!"*

William has also gone on to do voiceovers for the cartoon characters of Franklin and Arthur as well as commercials on radio and TV, and he is still at it.

The photo below is of Nicholas and William on the set of Murdock Mysteries.

Chapter One

A Good Cover Letter To Get An Agent Or Manager

When going for an agent or manager, you are going to need a cover letter. Here are my cover letter tips:

1/ Spell the person's name correctly. You wouldn't believe how many people mess up.

2/ Keep it down to 2 or 3 short paragraphs. Paragraph 1 is an introduction of who you are. Paragraph 2 is what you are about (new to the business etc.), and paragraph 3 is what you want from the person you are writing the letter to.

3/ Proof thoroughly. No spelling or grammar errors.

4/ Don't belittle yourself or your work. Example, don't say, "I was only an extra..." or "I don't have a lot of experience."

Turn it into a positive sentence like, *"I was fortunate to have been an extra on some amazing films like"* ...) or, *"my experience so far has prepared me to where I feel eager and ready to step up to the next level."* Also, if you can mention a few recent productions you've done.

5/ Remember, cover letters need to be professionally written, informative and compelling. It needs to also express you.

Most agents will read the cover letter, look at your photo and if they are still interested, they might look over your demo reel. This means that what you send in your package MUST make a strong impression.

Acting Scams

What a scam? Example, you go to see a photographer or an agent and they suggest that you take acting classes. Is this a scam you ask? It depends; did you ask the person for a recommendation? Did the topics just come up in conversation? Or perhaps you feel that you were "lured" into classes. Let's take a look at some of the scams and how they "lure" you into separating you from your money. Your eye catches an ad in a newspaper that a talent or modeling agency is looking for "new faces" – "no experience" needed, just show up for an interview, or an 'audition." They will tell you that they have booked new talent into lots of "contracts" and "jobs" to make you believe they are the real thing and that this is your chance of a lifetime!

HERE ARE THE DEAD GIVEAWAYS TO LOOK FOR: Reputable agencies don't have to put ads in the papers. Check to see if an agent secretly owns an Acting School. Oh yes! The rats own both and trick you, and I know this for a fact! How it works is when people go to the "agent" in the hope that this agent will take them on. This so-called "agent" sends them over to an "independent acting school" for training. If the agent recommends say, three schools, then that's better because they won't own all three, but if the agent only recommends you to one school – look out!

Over the years I personally came across a few agents who actually owed acting schools on the sly. And when they knew a sucker was coming to visit and learn about the so-called "agency", (which was also a scam – a front to lure the star-struck kids/parents into their web), the agent would take down any photos pertaining to the acting school and after the students left, the agent would put the photos back up again. It's a true story, and I have many more sordid stories I could write a real expose on... Hey, maybe I will.

Just be careful, when an "agency" claims to have launched the careers of famous people, they may only have had some brief affiliation with that celebrity or their agency. Genuine agencies would prefer that you already have acting training and are experienced enough to be able to perform well at auditions and land a role. Google the agent and see if they have a bad reputation. For example, try a term like "Modeling or acting agent scams in Toronto" or New York. You can even check the ACTRA "no cheque" list, and you will see some questionable agents on their list. Do your research.

Chapter One

Another scam is, are you ready to... "Get Discovered!!"

The scammers appear legitimate, complete with radio and television ads, professional "talent agents" in attendance and the promise of fame for the chosen few. All this "sizzle" is designed to get you in the door for the big sell.

The scammers set up their tables in a room at the hotel and have you turn up for an audition or an interview. During this time they will sometimes have you perform a simple TV commercial script on a camera. Then they tell you that you have good potential, that you have a good camera presence and great eyes for the camera. Then they tell you that they will get back to you in a few days, or so, to tell you if you have been accepted.

This is to make you sit on the edge of your seat for a few days simmering with anxiety. Then the phone rings and guess what, YOU HAVE BEEN ACCEPTED!!!

Now, they book you for an interview and tell you to bring both of your parents. The reason they want both of the parents at the interview with you is because the scammers have learned its best to "sell" both Mom and Dad together. Also, they don't want you to go home and think about it overnight because you will cool down and get wise to the scam. What the scammers do is get you "excited" right then and there, and then they get you to sign on the dotted line right away – that's how they get you. Then if you cool down the next day, and want a refund, sorry, that's not our policy. And that's just the start of the 'milking' process.

So far, you have paid perhaps $600 or 1800 dollars for photos or a course, but now they sell you on the extras, and then they move you onto the super sell. This could be a big event in North America or Canada that "everyone is going to." This is the opportunity for you to get discovered and be famous!! Here you get the chance to "showcase" your talents in singing, modeling, acting, TV commercials, print work or even the catwalk, etc, etc., etc.

The Actors Success In The Making

This is all designed to bring in thousands of young hopefuls and all their MONEY! Do the math, if you run one big event and get say 5000 young hopefuls to turn up, and each pays you $4,000 for all included. Multiply 5,000 hopefuls by 4,000 dollars, and you get TWENTY MILLION DOLLARS for five days work! Get the idea? Now it's true, a few people do get hired in real jobs, and 99.9% of the others don't even get a set of steak knives for all the money they spent. What they get are broken hearts — kids whose dreams are shattered. It's a disturbing reality. Now, have the same event run in another city, and you just made another TWENTY MILLION DOLLARS! And that's not all. Now you decide to do it all again somewhere else like LA, Milan, Miami, Toronto, or how about a big boat cruise!

At one event, I was a judge sitting beside other judges, and we the judges were watching young hopeful's step up on stage and perform their monologues. When we the judges took a break, I asked one of the judges seated with me at the judge's table, what he looks for in a performer when they are doing their monologue? He told me that he had no idea, he came from Europe representing a modeling agency, and for him, this was a free ticket to North America for a week of fun. (A true story).

You as the event owner would be raking in MILLIONS OF DOLLARS A YEAR. That's why the scammers do it. They live the life of kings, or should I say parasites off the hopes and dreams of the most innocent of all, our children. They deceive us out of our hard-earned money, and then break the hearts and spirits of our kids so that their kids can live the dream of opulence, wealth and brand name Italian handbags that cost 800 dollars – so coooooool!

Please do your research and Google "Acting or modeling scams."

Chapter Two

SPECIAL BONUS CHAPTER TWO

This next portion is from my book *"What's So Special About YOU?"* And the reason I have included this bonus chapter if you will is because of its true relevance to the actor or performer. For context: what you are about to read is about performing, and later you will read private journals from my students in their book *"Life Lessons From An Acting Class"* as they went through my nine weeks fulltime acting intensive. I have included this work into the book for you to learn to improve your game, so read on.

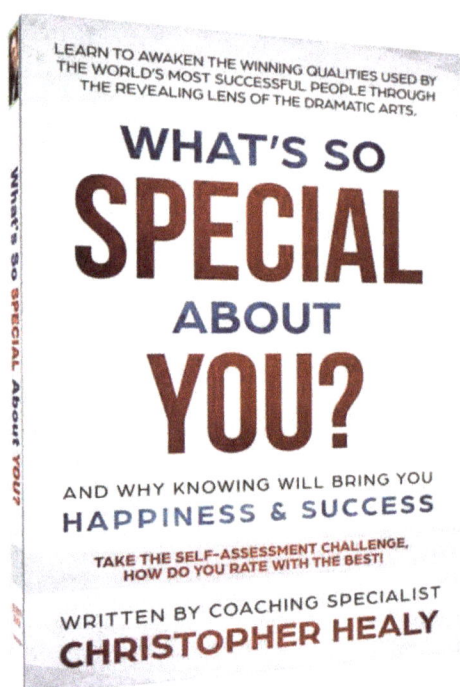

The Actors Success In The Making

All The World's A Stage

(Chapter 8)

"Personality always did, always does, and always will sell."
Christopher Healy – Coach, presenter, and author.

In the new economy where information content is "king" and your personality is gold, you need to face your fears of public speaking and look into the lens of the camera, so you can <u>communicate</u> to your followers, supporters, clients and customers.

Now that the Gladiatorial games had ended, the students could take a deep sigh of relief before tackling their next assignment - the "monologues."

Those of you who are new to acting may not have heard of the term "monologue." The Webster's dictionary definition of a monologue is a "dramatic sketch performed by one actor," and that can be any length from 1 – 5 minutes. Most monologues are about 2 minutes in length.

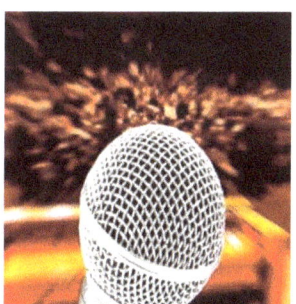
The most important thing about having a monologue prepared is allowing people to see your talent. It's also important to have if you're new to acting because your monologue is your calling card. Most agents and managers are on the lookout for experienced actors with work experience credits, but, may take on a newcomer who performs a monologue with an outstanding performance.

Learning a monologue is like learning a speech. It can feel overwhelming at times. Even to the most experienced executive, speaking in public may sometimes feel like they are climbing a mountain. When ready, you would walk out on

Chapter Two

stage in front of everyone watching you. You can hear a pin drop. Then you speak. Yikes!!

Monologues require your keen intuition, especially when trying to make decisions on how to play the text or what nuances to show behind the words.

For actors, having a good monologue prepared may be their ticket in for a manager or agent to discover them, and get them out into the world of show business.

However, for regular people, having an opportunity to tell someone about yourself can sometimes leave you "speechless," and how embarrassing is that?

It's well advised to work out in advance, what you would tell people about "you," and be prepared for when that opportunity may arise. I am not going to dig too deep into the art of communication except to say that, <u>spoken communication</u> is our most powerful form of persuasion and as such, its vital for not just actors, but for regular people, executives, managers, especially entrepreneurs to learn the art of **<u>PRESENTATION</u>.**

People, including actors, need to learn how to communicate with clarity, authentically, and with influence. I hope you can see how showing your genuine personality for presentations on stage or on camera can massively benefit you as an actor, businessperson, manager, employee and of course the entrepreneur.

To quote a successful man named Brendon Burchard who is the founder of "Experts Academy" and #1 New York Times and #1 USA Today bestselling author of ***"The Millionaire Messenger"*** and ***"The Charge"*** - <u>*"Speaking is the only way to get your message out there. Now more than ever, you are selected from others based on what you say, how you say it, how you appear, and how real and authentic you are."*</u>

And I will quote from another insightful book ***"Celebrity branding YOU"*** by Nick Nanton and J.W. Dicks. <u>*"People buy People'*</u>, meaning it's all about your personality.

So, the message is the same for all of us: Follow in the footsteps of the world's most successful people by learning to overcome your fears, hang-ups and self-doubts, and learn to be a master communicator. You will make great progress towards happiness and success.

Truth is that most people hate public speaking and most people can't stand how they look or sound, and have low self-esteem and so when they step up on stage or on camera or any public forum they feel dread inside because they are being seen. They believe that by being seen and heard they may embarrass themselves and look like a fool and they feel that they would die of shame, because in truth, they aren't worthy.

So bottom line for most people is that they settle for second best in most everything they do and say and believe and strive for. In this regard, are you like most people? Because if you are then I feel sorry for you. Please listen to me when I tell you that YOU need to change now, improve yourself now!

Here is the secret to success: *If you want to be a success in anything, business, careers, relationships, especially in life, then you had better learn how to **communicate effectively.*** Meaning: ***clearly, authentically, with passion and with influence.***

That's it.

If you can't communicate clearly what you are thinking, or feeling, or if you can't communicate clearly your decisions, opinions, ideas or whatever you want done effectively to the person beside you, then you are lost.

Trust me: learn to feel worthy of yourself, to have confidence in YOU and learn how to communicate clearly, authentically, with passion and with influence and *YOU WILL THRIVE!*

Chapter Two

Therefore, the best advice I can offer anyone in business including actors is to take courses in the following:

- Public Speaking
- On stage presentations
- Being interviewed and giving interviews
- Presenting at sales meetings and conferences
- Online webinars and courses
- Direct to camera video presentations
- Speeches and business pitches
- Presenting "shopping channel" style
- Presenting for Infomercials
- Doing TV commercials, even mock-up commercials.
- Speaking at media interviews
- Speaking for "coaching style."
- Speaking for DVD's
- Presenting "news broadcasting style."
- Walking into the room introductions
- Working on your image – how do you want to be seen?
- Take courses on inner healing of self. If you don't heal the inside, then your fears and hang-ups (about the way you look or sound) are still making you tense on camera. When on the camera you want to be relaxed, letting your personality shine. If you are not relaxed, then your personality will not fully shine through to impress others in a positive light. Finally, about the training list above, try some of them just to break out of being the typical, old you.

For example, in my twenty plus years of teaching acting, I had in my classes all types of men and women, from ex-Russian soldiers, doctors, nurses, accountants, electricians, psychologists, university students, bankers, entrepreneurs, writers, directors, a prison guard and of course actors. All had their own reasons to try something new, and all wanted to improve their lives. Most were willing to learn, get up and try, while others just wanted me to be their babysitter. Do yourself a favor and go try something new from the list I provided you above. Go empower yourself.

Let's see if any of the seven empowering qualities on the next page from the world's most successful people are able to engage you into breaking out of your old mold. On the next page are success qualities from the world's most successful people. When filling out your answers be honest. The boxes range from the MOST on the far left to the LEAST or not good at it then place a tick in the box on the far right. Good luck.

Chapter Two

How do you rate with the best
ROUND 8

Successful people tend to be or have:

55/Communicators: They understand that *"communication in all its forms"* are powerful keys to success and happiness. However, this quality of "communication skills" drills deeper down to being *"articulate"* - speaking so that you are clearly understood is absolutely critical to your success. Articulate people know how to get to the point. Being articulate promotes their capacity of intelligentsia, education, culture, confidence and the higher echelons of potential leadership. There is almost a *"statesmanship"* like polish to this quality, and it is impressive. They can express thoughts, ideas, or feelings **coherently from their mind to you**, so you can understand exactly what they are thinking, which brings clarity to whatever the situation is. [How effective a communicator (not just a talker) are you?]

56/Tenacious: Meaning, they are a strategic thinker who possess a will that refuses to submit. They will hold fast while making adjustments to achieve success. [How tenacious are you when the going gets tough?]

57/Excellent Listeners: To again pin point another form of effective communication we turn to "Listening." The world's most successful people know how to be silent and let others share their opinions. For them, being the loudest person in the room is not what being successful is about. When they listen to another person, they don't hold their breath, waiting to find a spot to jump in with their thoughts. They are mindful, attentive and present with and to the other person speaking because they truly want to know and understand. [How good are you at listening, not just pretending to listen?]

The Actors Success In The Making

58/Persuasive: They know that if you can't get somebody to "Yes" then the exercise is a non-starter. So they have learned to apply all their qualities, skills and charms to the art of persuading somebody to say "Yes." [How effective are you at getting people to say "Yes"?]

59/Friendly: They create a pleasant and welcoming atmosphere through their character, their homes, at work and in their lives. [How friendly are you to create a welcoming atmosphere?]

60/Open-Minded: They are open minded enough to change their viewpoints, opinions or decisions according to circumstances. They stay open-minded and not closed off in a rut. Nothing for them is set in stone. [How open-minded are you?]

61/Wellbeing: They know that a peaceful body and mind allows for creativity, innovation, decision making, and opens a channel for their wisdom and intuitive insight. They exercise daily and meditate their minds, allowing for the renewal of body, mind and spirit. [How well do you look after your health?]

What's your score for round 8?

From the total of 7 questions, tally up and give yourself a 1, 2, 3, 4, or 5 for each tick you placed in the appropriate box as below.

By the way, the highest score was 7. Can you see where you are on par with the world's most successful people and where you need to make more self-improvements to become truly successful? Remember, talent is what you start, with so get to work on improving any of the above success qualities, and your life will improve for the better.

Chapter Two

This next portion is from the book, *"Life Lessons From An Acting Class"*.

Apart from the monologues that the students had to do for this week, we also covered the promotional Demo reel. A promotional DVD of 3 – 5 minutes in length of the actor's work is a critical tool for their self-promotional package. Actors would send their promotional DVD's (with photo and resume) to agents so they can see what the actor looks like on camera, and how talented they are and then hopefully, sign them up for representation. Actors also use their promotional DVD to get acting work from casting directors, producers and directors.

The DVD's I made for my students would showcase them with memorable, assorted dynamic "looks", reaction shots, compelling scenes and a relaxed personal "on camera" interview that best <u>sells who that person is and who they could be</u> to agents, personal managers, casting directors, producers and directors.

For my students, this was the most demanding part of the course because in order to get excellent quality for the DVD's, we need real production. We need real cameras, lights, and plenty of re-shoots until they get it right. Also, the scenes that the students have chosen to perform must be right for them in showcasing their best qualities. It's the real deal now, and more than ever I need to see each of them relaxed on camera, showcasing their inspiring personalities.

Now.., it's SHOWTIME! **FOR CONTEXT:** The movie of the week we watched for character analysis was:

IN THE PURSUIT OF HAPPINESS

This is an astoundingly true rags-to-riches story!

Will Smith plays Chris Gardner a father struggling to take care of his young son in this touching true story. In San Francisco in 1981, Chris Gardner's (Smith) luck has run out. A bad business investment, a bevy of parking tickets, and back taxes in addition to rent, childcare, and groceries keep him constantly scrambling for cash.

Chris thinks his luck is changing when he is accepted into a highly competitive internship program at a brokerage firm. But the internship is unpaid and soon, despite his best efforts, Chris and his five-year-old son, Christopher (Jaden Christopher Syre Smith--Will Smith's real-life son), find themselves homeless. Chris might spend his days training to invest and make millions, but he and Christopher spend their nights in homeless shelters, sleeping in washrooms, and public transportation stations.

Gardner's story is a TRUE testament not only of the love between a father and son, but also to the strength of the human spirit. Chris Gardner is a man who NEVER gave in to despair, and made an astonishing transformation from being part of the city's invisible poor to being a powerful player in its financial district.

And it's also a book! "Pursuit of Happiness: From the Mean Streets to Wall Street" by Chris Gardner.

Chapter Two

OPENING THE JOURNALS

"WHAT DID YOU LEARN FROM TODAY AND HOW DID YOU GROW FROM WHAT YOU LEARNED?'

DAY 29 ~ Suppressed emotions can absolutely destroy a person

We are preparing to shoot our DVD shortly, and part of that DVD is an on-camera interview. We have had to write out and memorize our lines, and at the end of the interview, I am supposed to say a one-liner that will leave the viewer with a positive and lasting impression of me. So, because I had to come up with about 30 different one-liners expressing how I feel about acting before one was finally approved, it has remained on my mind for some time. "Acting cultivates my creativity" is certainly true, yet I'm still not satisfied. Since I can't elaborate on it in the one-liner, I will elaborate on it here, for myself, so I never forget it.

The creation aspect is vital, but mentioning only the creativity emphasizes the pretending involved in acting; it fails to mention the truths. I act because it gives me the freedom and courage to feel. To truly feel and not to fake it. And yes, sometimes these feelings are strongly negative ones, as in the anguish, fear, and frustration that Mr. Healy drew out of me yesterday for my dramatic monologue. When I tell this to my friends, they look at me with eyes like little beads. They understand that feeling truthfully is what makes a scene good, but most of them don't understand why I would enjoy reliving such dark emotions.

However, one friend does understand, and this is the friend who has gone through therapy. Therein lies my explanation. In therapy, the first and most important step taken by the therapist is getting the patient to be open about how they feel. Suppressed emotions can absolutely destroy a person. But when you're open, accepting and self-aware of them, they can't hide and fester in dark corners of your mind and build into a monster that you're not even conscious of. Acting keeps me away from denial, it shows me that my mind is strong enough to put itself into hell, and then bring itself right back, safe and sound. This above all, I value about my art.

Tab was absent Day 30

DAY 31 ~ Everyone knows the self-loathing feeling of knowing you can do something but failing to do it

Today I experienced the frustration of forgetting a direction and then having no chance to redeem myself. Yesterday Mr. Healy gave me directions to follow for my comedic monologue, and in performing it today, I didn't integrate a single one of them. When I was finished, Healy gave me a look and said "What happened to the towel? The mirror? The hair flip?" Remembering, I said "Oh, right, sorry," and prepared to do it again, properly this time. Only I didn't get to do it again. Mr. Healy ejected my tape and sent me away. His teaching schedule was tight, and everyone had one chance to get it right, and I blew it.

Everyone knows the self-loathing feeling of knowing you can do something but failing to do it, and the feeling of "if only I'd been reminded of this detail before my performance," or "if only they'd watch me do it one more time." But I can only blame myself for being ill-prepared, for not looking over my notes one last time. This is a mistake I cannot afford to make in more serious situations. I can't waste people's time like this. I need to be more professional and learn the "discipline" of all that I am learning here.

And how about in the real world, when the boss asks me to get this, and have that prepared for the next meeting, and I turn up with – "oh, I forgot." Life may be about second chances, but auditions and performances are not. Tomorrow I will take my directions more seriously.

DAY 32 ~ I must listen to that little voice inside myself

I learned about thinking like an entrepreneur in all sorts of aspects of life, not just career ambitions. The story of how Mr. Healy met and married his wife inspired me, not only to go and propose to someone literally a day after meeting them but to balance thinking tactically with following gut instinct. In too many instances I have disregarded impulses in favor of only cold, calculating thought. In this way, I have convinced myself to stay in relationships that have gone cold, taken actions opposed to what I wanted to do because I thought it would be wiser.

However, putting my music degree on a hiatus, leaving my home in BC, and moving to Toronto to pursue my acting is an instance where I managed to ignore the pedantic little voice in my head and follow my heart. This is a path I intend to keep following, especially when listening to the stories from Mr. Healy. But to be effective, this way of life does have to be coupled with a business-oriented and tactical mind. I must be steered by professionalism, fueled by passion and listen to that little voice inside myself.

DAY 29 ~ I need to be able to push past this and focus on what needs to get done

Today my head wasn't in it. Hard as I tried nothing was sinking in. I was hearing critique, understanding it, but doing nothing with it. I need to be able to push past this and focus on what needs to get done. My two monologue choices have very different types of energy, which is going to take a lot of work to achieve. I picked them knowing they would be challenging and unfortunately today I wasn't ready for it. I plan to enter tomorrow with a new energy and approach to both scripts. I need to leave problems at the door and get the most out of our short time left with the program.

DAY 30 ~ The last thing I want to do is take the safe route

Today I brought different emotions and ideas to my monologues. In my mind, I had my own way of playing them and each way was safe. These monologues are meant to showcase my abilities, and the last thing I want to do is take the safe route. I like the idea of adding layers to our characters. Personalities are not built in a day, and by adding one layer at a time, we are strengthening our performances and understanding who we are portraying. Characters need depth, and this takes me back to the "knowing." The audience doesn't need to know everything about your character, but the actor does. And while certain aspects may never come out in the form of words, just the act of "knowing" conveys a message to the audience and adds a layer of familiarity and realism to the performance.

Chapter Two

DAY 31 ~ I've now started to embrace the ups and downs of everyday life

A director can't make you feel. They can prompt emotions, give you a mark, walk you through the motions, but they can't change what you are thinking. That part is up to you. You need to know who you are looking at and talking to; you need to visualize it so that the audience sees it. I generally hide my true emotions and put on a smile; it's one of my defense mechanisms. If nothing's wrong, I don't have to face it or deal with it.

When playing a character, I'm forced to show emotions I may not normally let myself express. Although it's a great way to release, I often have a hard time relating to the character and drawing from my own personal experiences. I've now started to embrace the ups and downs of everyday life. I have begun to live emotions and see them as a reaction of the entire body. My challenge now is to channel that into stillness. Doing less is more on camera and emotions are not weakness, but strength.

DAY 32 ~ I learned to just breathe and keep it simple

Today I was surprised. We filmed our angry and sad looks for our DVD promotional reel and the thought of capturing those emotions in a few seconds would have seemed impossible. I kept telling myself that I needed words to express emotions, even though the entire course I have been reminded it's not about the lines. It's about the reactions and the feelings.

Today that idea really showed that without words we have created different "looks" through expression and body language. The breathing is what helped me the most: remembering to keep subtle movement in the emotions, kept me focused and in the moment. I learned to just breathe and keep it simple.

The Actors Success In The Making

DAY 29 ~ Experiences are golden treasures

I can't believe, we're almost at the end of the course and that we're actually beginning our last stage. My mind is full of so many things as I ask myself "What did I learn today and how did I grow?" Today I caught myself being scared exposing myself through the character of my dramatic monologue. I chose a particular monologue because it has a very deep and personal meaning to me. I truly feel it; I've been there because I know what it feels like to be betrayed and hurt by the one you love so much.

I know how portraying my character in my dramatic monologue feels from beginning to end and still when I went through it with Mr. Healy, all I did was restrain myself, from getting hurt, by bringing all those memories of being cheated on by my boyfriend back to life. In result, the monologue was just lines, and there was no reality in them. Who'd have thought, that after seven weeks of hearing how acting is not pretending or saying lines, but expressing our true selves with the characters, I'd still be doing it? I caught myself being fearful. "Well, I'm sorry dear Ana, but if you really want to enjoy that monologue, to connect to people and to be real, then you've gotta let go of the fear of getting hurt." I'll leave that to normal people because for actors; these experiences are golden treasures that should be enjoyed through our performances.

Chapter Two

DAY 30 ~ Success comes through hard work

Today is not exactly about what did I learn, but more about, what I'm learning. I'm still learning to relax into a simple stillness for my on-camera performances, and let my eyes share everything with the camera, instead of constantly making little moves here and there that cause distraction. This process is hard to do, but I'm working on it; learning to separate theatre from film. And as I work in this technicality, I'm simultaneously working with my character. I'm learning to have patience through the process, and keep a positive attitude. If there is something through life I've learned, it's that success comes through hard work.

DAY 31 ~ "Very difficult" does not equal impossible

I felt more confident about my dramatic monologue performance because the night before I practiced it with less distracting movement. Nonetheless, to my surprise, when I practiced it in front of the camera, I was still moving a lot, and then I understood that I have to be STILL, as in not moving eyebrows, smacking/licking lips – just simple stillness. Just me being simply in the moment, allowing myself to express the whole monologue through my eyes. WOW! Now, everything gets much harder. This is not just a technicality of theatre, but part of me. After 18 yrs of moving cheeks, eyebrows, lips, forehead... just everything in my face, I have to make still, all these movements that cause distraction in a close up on camera. Yesterday, I thought that removing theatricality was hard... well; today it's definitely much more difficult. Yes, it's going to be very difficult but "very difficult" does not equal impossible... and "very difficult" doesn't stop me from pursuing my dreams.

DAY 32 ~ Little by little, through perseverance, I'm getting there

Today, I was the first to perform my dramatic monologue. It is still hard for me, to stay still and just express through my eyes, the little details, the anger, the frustration, etc... But, little by little, through perseverance, I'm getting there.

This makes me learn again, that even in the little things, one must be persistent! Keep eyes focused on the goal.

DAY 29 ~ Ditch the stress and leave panic at home

There is no better way to feel more at ease with your performance than to be prepared. Even when you're just rehearsing, when you are fully aware of what you're doing and come in with your project ready, everything becomes more fun, and you're much easier to work with. You ditch the stress and leave panic at home.

These last two weeks are crucial to coming in prepared, and I learned this yesterday as I was too focused on getting my lines perfect instead of feeling what my character should be feeling. Even on days like today where I feel I haven't learned anything, there are lessons too small to realize in the moment. However as we continue through life, we become more aware of them as we need them.

DAY 30 ~ It's the subtle differences that create a huge change

The day draws nearer where we will finish up our last class and head back home. Each day we are detaching more from this place that we called home for the past two months and from a man that describes himself as the village idiot. I am excited and nervous as to what is out there, but we have learned so much I don't even know where to start.

I was thinking about it tonight while on the bus ride home; then noticed a change in myself, in everything I do, and yes we have the tools, but they would render useless if we weren't built up to where we are now. I am so different than when I first started this course, not physically of course but mentally and emotionally, for it's the subtle differences that create a huge change. There have been times like today where I'll be feeling a bit down, but someday I'll look back at this book and times like this and laugh, and that's an attitude I developed while being here, because I'm learning what I can do and I'll continue to break free.

DAY 31 ~ This all develops over time with practice, practice, practice

Become who you are? Such a strange statement. You would think that you're the master at who you are and your emotions, but something happens when we know we're on display. We must go back to the place the emotion came from, not just remembering the time, but go back in and linger in that moment and re-live the experience, handling it as our character would. The challenge is to stay focused enough that you make yourself believe who you are and where you're living in your mind. This "focus" is absolutely crucial to your success; I can't say it enough.

We must be comfortable enough and focused to just sit there and let the emotions come to us Allow movements so subtle that can ready your thoughts. Actors learn to feel emotions and transform their way of seeing something happy or sad to create a story in their eyes. This emotional sight in the eyes allows the audience to get connected with you on an intimate level as if it were their own lives. I have learned that this all develops over time with practice, practice, practice. The more you borrow from your memories, the easier it becomes to experience your emotions. This, in turn, liberates you from any suppressed emotions or allows you to feel emotions as never before in a safe, playful way.

DAY 32 ~ It's important to bring the real you, wherever you go in life

As we learn of self-promotion and wrap up with the business side of acting, I see the days flying by. We are one step closer to entering the world. I'm really excited, but I would be lying if I said I'm not nervous, or that I'm not going to

The Actors Success In The Making

miss this class. I keep thinking about home and how different it's going to be. I have a whole new perspective on things now. If I have taken away anything from Mr. Healy's course, it would be, "that it's important to bring the real you, wherever you go in life." We mustn't put the masks back on that we worked 2 1/2 months to strip away. I know it will be hard to get used to the lack of routine, but now that we have the knowledge it's our job to take what we have learned and develop ourselves. Find our own routine. Some of us may only make it so far, some of us may not make it at all, but the others will move forward into their dreams and make an impression on people, out there, and live the success we have indulged in for a lifetime and so vividly over the course. I will continue visualizing what I want because I know that when I push myself through the things that scare me the most; I'm driving me closer to where I want to be.

DAY 29 ~ Stop and really look at what success is to you and how you plan on getting there

I learned that it is important to not allow stress and fears cloud your desires for what you want. What you need is a clear idea of what you truly want and why.

It is important to stop and really look at what success is to you, and how you plan on getting there. When you put your full effort and energy into something, you have to have a drive behind it, and you have to be completely clear on what that drive and desire is. Once you have a focus and understanding of a true and deep reason for what you want, you will have a better chance of achieving it, but only if you take the action of doing so.

Chapter Two

DAY 30 ~ You need to be the one who gets you out of bed in the morning

I was reminded of how important it is to take control of your own reality; no one else is going to care about your future or career as much as you do. You need to be the one who gets you out of bed in the morning; no one else will do it for you. It doesn't matter how amazing or beneficial your dreams are unless you choose to make them happen, after all, they are only dreams unless you put continuous conscious effort into making them a reality.

Trying to push your life forward in such a competitive industry filled with highly talented people can become numbing. Becoming discouraged and depleted can make you want to back off and return to pretending and hoping for the world to change, and give you everything you want, but that will never happen. We cannot chase what is not there; we have to create it first. To create and manifest my own reality, and take charge of where my future is going, is what I choose to focus on. I understand I need to have a clear vision and push forwards in my life, and not become distracted because I know I am the only one who can truly create my own happiness and success or my own misery.

DAY 31 ~ You can't lose sight of what you want

As our days get closer to the end of the course, I am becoming more aware of what we really need to have, to be prepared for the future. I feel I have grown so much in my understanding and practice in acting, but I have always had the safety net of the classroom. It's one thing to understand a script and how to become a character, but I haven't actually tried acting in the real world.

Now I have to be prepared and organized to put everything in place before I even get the chance to do what we do in class. Acting is not just a hobby or a fun activity; I want to make it my career. I need to be fully focused and not lose myself in distractions or boredom. Throughout this course, I have learned that you can't lose sight of what you want, and that is so important to be aware of where you are in life.

DAY 32 ~ We now have to design our own future

Soon we will be stepping into audition rooms full of people we don't know, in places we don't know, trying to find our way on new ground. We became use to the structure of a 10:30 to 5:30 day, daily journals, scenes, lines to memorize, etc. But soon we won't have the guidance and motivation of our teacher Mr. Healy, or the constant acting practice we have now. In a week we will have to move along on our own. It's terribly important to remember what we have learned and how we have changed. To not get lost in the distractions we will meet every day. To not allow ourselves to become stagnant because we now have to design our own future and we can't rely on someone else to do it for us.

DAY 29 ~ Stop the doubt and just do it

We spent some time working on our monologues, and I was pretty nervous to begin working on my dramatic one. Emotional and dramatic roles have always been my weakness. I always find it so difficult to get into the mindset of somebody else who is very upset or angry, but I realized today that maybe that's because I've never fully allowed myself to do so. Being obscure and funny is what I love to do; it's my strong point, so I never really cared to push myself to do anything else. After rehearsing my dramatic monologue, I think I actually did a decent job because I stopped worrying about sucking and just did it.

I want to be an actor that can play any role, not just be funny. And the only way I can make that happen is if I stop the doubt and just do it.

Chapter Two

DAY 30 ~ I am moving along in the right direction

After rehearsing our monologues over and over I thought that it was going to get boring and repetitive, but I realized today just how much rehearsing and practicing really helps.

I think a lot of the time we abuse the rehearsal time we get, we get bored easily and figure we've done it enough times and so our performance will be great, but there's always something that needs to be fixed to make it just right. This is not about perfection but is it about turning over every little stone to learn more of who you character is.

I thought I had been doing my monologues fine, but then I learned that like always, I am talking super-fast. I never even noticed I'm doing it half the time until I watched myself on TV and I sounded like I was permanently on fast forward. I think everyone has their own little habit or thing they always do, and talking fast is mine, but I don't want it to consume my performance or ruin my ability to act. After doing a couple of exercises that Mr. Healy gave me to practice I became more aware of what I was doing, and the exercises helped me to slow down my speaking. After performing the monologue again later on, it was way better and slower. I feel like, as in real life, that I am moving along in the right direction, but it takes focus and hard, constant, work.

DAY 31 ~ When I try, I can accomplish anything

We again rehearsed our monologues in the morning and when performing my comedy one I was able to finally slow down and talk like a normal person. Not only did this make my performance better, but it felt good to know that when I try, I can accomplish anything.

Another thing I was able to conquer today was to finally cry. It's been a struggle for me since the beginning to make myself cry, and I would just give up on it. But once again I accomplished something I never thought I could do. With clear guidance from Mr. Healy, I was able to trust, as he guided me with the precision of a surgeon, into a dark place.

Although it hurt to have to go to such a deep and painful place, but I'm glad I did, and now I know where I have to go emotionally and mentally, for not only this monologue but future scenes too. It's liberating.

Caitlin was absent Day 32

DAY 29 ~ Take control of your life by taking action

We're coming up on the last final sprint of the journey to the center of ourselves. I learned today that leadership is something that I need to have with my career because when it comes down to it, the only person who has control over my life is me. Your agents love, and admiration for you is only as good as your next gig that subsidizes their negotiated 20%; which is why it's imperative to build relationships with people who have your best interests at heart. It's also important to take control of your life by taking action, because you know better than anyone, what you want for yourself and what you need for yourself.

I grew from this knowing that I have real leadership within myself. I can't help but feel a little scared that the class is ending and I don't know if I'll be able to apply what I've learned in the real world. But hey, you know what else I learned, that the words "I don't know" haven't existed for me for the past two months. I've come this far without needing them.

Chapter Two

DAY 30 ~ I'm not hoping and waiting for things to happen, I'm making them happen

I feel liberated. I don't know how to explain it, but I just feel that everything is getting a lot easier and a lot more fun. Anything worth doing is worth doing right, and I did both my monologues today without any uncertainty or worry at all. I owe this to the last two months of training that has completely changed my way of thinking for the better. I'm not hoping and waiting for things to happen, I'm making them happen. I grew from this today by embracing what I have done for myself compared to what I was doing to myself before. Now that I understand the realities of both sides of the coin, I can now be purposeful with my passion without any hindrance.

DAY 31 ~ If you take life too seriously you'll never get out alive

I'd rather be safe than sorry is a very popular saying. However, when it comes to acting, I'd rather be sorry than safe. Playing it safe in acting is like smoking a cigarette at the gas station: not only is it ill-advised but it's dangerous. Acting without risk is like no acting at all, and the same principle applies to life.

I learned today after going through my monologues that I'm truly proud of what I do. This wonderful feeling has spread throughout my entire body, and now it's flowing through me like the blood in my veins. It motivates me to push beyond my limits and have some fun doing that. I'm going to focus on what comes around for me today. Just one day at a time because today is the first day of the rest of my life and if you take life too seriously you'll never get out alive.

DAY 32 ~ Heighten the qualities about yourself and use them to your advantage

I learned the important values of marketing myself and the entrepreneurial side of being an actor because being an actor isn't just about acting, it's about selling something, and that something is you. This is a business, and I am the product. So it's imperative that you heighten the qualities about yourself and use them to your advantage in order to sell yourself the best way that you can. I grew from this today by understanding and appreciating that acting alone is only half of the journey. I need to think like a businessman in terms of promoting myself and establishing a business-work-ethic.

END OF WEEK 8 IN REVIEW

Wow, what a week for the students, it seems like they were hit with everything including the kitchen sink. Did you notice aside from their <u>inner conflicts</u> about moving on in the real world, that most of their "one-liners" at the top of their journals were very pro-active adjectives, descriptive words, which inspire action, reward, and affirmations.

Words like *"Experience great treasures, push past this and focus, ditch the stress, take control of your life with action, breathe, heighten the qualities about yourself, stop and really look at what success really is to you, balance thinking critically with following your gut instinct."*

All of what these students have feared throughout this adventure fell away, only to make way for new fears, new unknown challenges to come.

The difference now is that each of them now **believes** that whatever life throws at them, they have the tools that will allow them to <u>be capable of pushing through</u> and keep themselves on their own path to happiness and success. Isn't this what we all want to know in our own hearts?

This is a huge change in these kids' lives, and they can feel it. This change will stay with them for the rest of their lives and hopefully inspire others to live their dreams to the fullest.

My favorite line was from Tab when she said: *"I must listen to that inner voice inside myself."* So true!

Chapter Two

My two questions to you are: Do you believe in you? Do you listen to your inner voice?

This then concludes the special chapter from the books ***"What's So Special About You?"***

and ***"Life Lessons From An Acting Class."***

I hope they gave you greater insight into the minds of people and of course, actors. I trust you will learn from it and grow from what you have learnt. You can review those books by going to the website: **www.ChristopherHealy.ca**

CHAPTER THREE

WHEN YOU GET TO THE "SET"

Judging from the end credits, a feature film unit has a bewildering number of roles and an army of people. The role descriptions that follow are confined to the modest core likely to carry out the low-budget film or video shoot. Familiarize yourself with who you would be on set with.

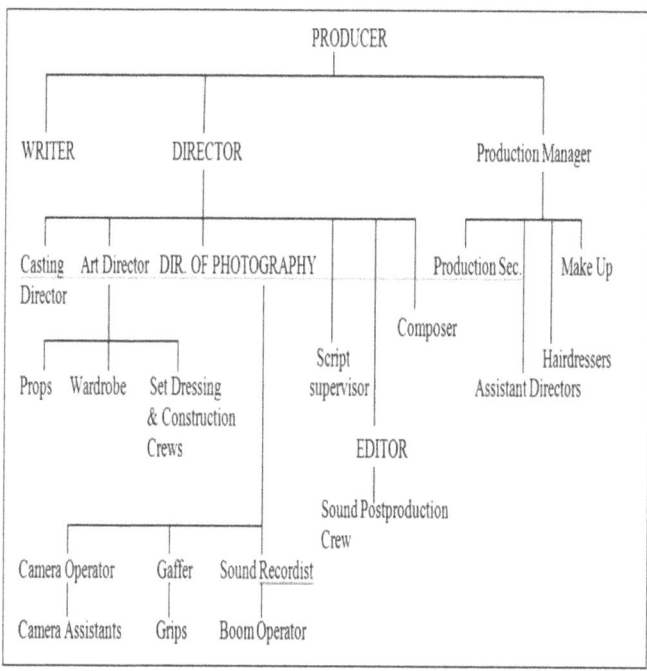

PRODUCER: Answerable to Investors or studio heads. Responsibilities: the producer of a film assembles and administers the necessary funds, and oversees the project as a whole. Traditionally, the producer also has ultimate say in an artistic dispute between, say, a principal actor and the director. Since status is defined by a number of factors, relative influence may be unconventional, and the producer must arbitrate such problems. Since the producer's role is primarily fiscal and logistical, he has under him the production department, consisting of assistant producer, production manager, production secretary, and assistant directors. Producers sometimes have assistants called Assistant Producers.

DIRECTOR: Answerable to The Producer. Responsibilities: The director is responsible for nothing less than the quality and meaning of the final film. This means writing or working with writers, researching locations, auditioning actors, and assembling a cast and crew. The director develops both cast and script through rehearsals, supervises the shooting schedule, directors' actors and crew during shooting, and later supervises the editing and finalization of the project. If there are no profits in view, the film may have no separate producer, so the director must additionally assemble funding before the making of the film and hustle distribution afterwards.

DIRECTOR OF PHOTOGRAPHY: Answerable to The director. Responsibilities: also known as lighting cameraperson, the director of photograph (DP) is the most important person in the crew after the director and is responsible for the look of the film. That is, he or she collaborates closely with the director and takes all decisions about camera, lighting, and equipment that contribute to the camerawork. The DP is also the leader of the whole crew and will often direct their work while the director concentrates on the actors. In the minimal crew the DP is responsible for specifying the lighting and camera equipment, lenses, film stock, or their video equivalents.

He or she is responsible for testing and adjusting that equipment and for being thoroughly conversant with its working principles. No important work should ever be done without running tests as early as possible in order to forestall Murphy's Law, which is inexorable in filmmaking. The DP decides and supervises the placement of lighting instruments and on a small crew reconnoiters each location in advance with the gaffer to assess electrical supplies and lighting design.

CAMERA OPERATOR: Answerable to The director of photography. Responsibilities: The operator is responsible for the handling of the camera, which means he or she takes an active role in deciding camera positioning (in collaboration with the director), and physically controls the camera movements such as panning, tilting, zooming in and out, and dollying (Technical terms and their significance are explained in the Glossary). It is also an advantage if your operator is alert to the many behavioral nuances that reveal character. In improvisation work or in documentary, the camera work is often "grab-shooting" so the operator must decide moment to moment what to shoot in a busy scene. While the director sees content happening three-dimensionally in front of (or sometimes behind) the camera, the operator sees the action in its framed, cinematic form. The director may redirect the camera to a different area, but much of the time the operator alone knows exactly what the action will look like on the screen. The director must, therefore, be able to place considerable reliance upon the operator's discrimination, and this is also true for very controlled framing and composition since movement within the frame often requires immediate and spontaneous adjustment of the camera's framing.

CAMERA ASSISTANTS: Answerable to the camera operator. Responsibilities: On a feature film there may be more than one assistant cinematographer (AC). Division of labor makes one a clapper operator and magazine loader, and another whose job it is to manually follow focus when the distance changes between subject and camera. ACs keep the camera optics and film gate clean manhandle the camera equipment from place to place. Their main requirements are to be highly organized, reliable, and zealous at maintaining the camera in prime condition, whether it is film or videotape. Because their responsibilities are almost wholly technical, it is more important they be good and diligent technicians. On a small unit, one camera assistant often does all the ancillary work, though this can lead to costly holdups.

Chapter Three

GAFFER AND GRIPS: Answerable to the director of photography. Responsibilities: The job of the gaffer is to rig lighting and to know how to go about doing anything that needs to be fixed, mounted, moved, pushed, lifted, or lowered. The gaffer must have a good grasp of mechanical and electrical principles in order to improve solutions for which there is no available piece of equipment. A good gaffer also understands not only the lighting instruments but the principles and practice of lighting itself, because he or she must be able to quickly grasp the meaning of the DP's lighting instructions. The job of the grip is to fetch and carry and to rig lighting according to the gaffer's instructions. He or she also has the highly skilled and coordinated job of moving the camera support (dolly, crane, truck, etc.) from mark to mark as the camera takes mobile shots. Grips should be strong, practical, organized, and willing. On the minimal crew, they may double to help with sound equipment, to fetch or deliver while shooting is in progress.

A skilled grip knows something about everyone's job and is capable of standing in for some technicians in an emergency.

SOUND RECORDIST AND BOOM OPERATOR: Answerable to the director of photography. Responsibilities: in the inexperienced crew the unfailing casualty is sound quality. Capturing clear, clean and consistent sound is either deceptively skilled or sound recording does not have the glamour to induce people to try. Probably both are true. Another obstacle is that even quiet expensive video recorders have a propensity for picking up ever known electrical interference. It is the sound recordist's responsibility to check sound and videotape equipment in advance and to solve malfunction problems as they arise. The boom operator's job is to place the microphone as close to sound sources as possible, without getting the mic in the shot or creating shadows. In a complicated dialogue scene, this means moving the mic around to catch each new speaker.

PRODUCTION MANAGER: Answerable to the producer. Responsibilities: The production manager (PM) might be considered a hard-to-find luxury on a minimal crew, but there are many people whose business background equips them to do this vital job surpassingly well. The PM is the producer's delegate and closely concerned with preproduction and production. He or she is a business manager who is based in an office and takes care of all the arrangements for the shoot. These might include finding overnight accommodations, booking rented equipment to the specifications of camera and sound people, making up (with the director) a shooting schedule, negotiating travel arrangements, and locating restaurants near the shoot. The PM will watch cash flow and incubate contingency plans in case bad weather stymies exterior shooting. He or she will hustle to prepare the way ahead. All this lightens the load on the director for whom such things are a distraction from controlling the performances and visualizing the film as it evolves.

ASSISTANT DIRECTOR: Answerable to the production manager. Responsibilities: On a feature shoot there may be a first, second, and third AD. Assistant Directors seldom become directors since their skills are organizational rather than artistic and lean toward production management. Their job is to do all the legwork and take care of all the logistical needs of the production. Scheduling, crowds, and doing the director's barking all come within the AD's purview. Sometimes in a director's absence, an AD will rehearse actors, but only if he or she has a strong grasp of the director's intentions. The experienced AD may direct the second unit, but this more often falls to the editor.

SCRIPT SUPERVISOR: Answerable to the director. Responsibilities: The script supervisor (also called continuity supervisor) must understand how the film will be edited together, and during shooting must continuously monitor what words, actions, props, and costumes are in use from shot to shot.

Shooting on videotape makes checking a relatively simple (though time-consuming) matter, but with film, no such record is visible until the rushes have been processed. And eagle-eyed observer who keeps a record will match another. The script supervisor also assists the director by ensuring there is adequate coverage of each scene, and when time or resources must be saved, is able to define what can be omitted or shortened.

ART DIRECTOR: Answerable to the director. Responsibilities: To design everything possible in the film's environment to effectively interpret the script. This means overseeing props and costumes, as well as managing the interior design of sets and locations. If the film is a period production, the art director will research the epoch and its social customs to ensure that costumes and decor are accurate and make an impact. On a low-budget movie, the art director will do his or her own set dressing, while on a larger production there is a special person, the set dresser, to take care of this responsibility.

WARDROBE & PROPS: Answerable to the art director. Responsibilities: Wardrobe and props' jobs are to locate, store, and maintain costumes and properties (objects such as ashtrays, baby toys, or grand pianos that dress the set). When no wardrobe person is available, each actor becomes responsible for his own costumes. The AD should double check beforehand what clothes each actor must bring for the next scene, so today's costume is not still in the actor's laundry basket.

MAKEUP AND HAIRDRESSING: Answerable to the production manager. Responsibilities: The people in makeup and hairdressing produce the appropriate physical appearance in face and hair, often with careful attention to period details.

A hidden part of the job is catering to actors' insecurities by helping them believe in the way they look. Where the character demands negative traits, the makeup artist may have to work against an actor's resistance.

Makeup is particularly tricky; directors should shoot tests to make sure the makeup looks credible and is compatible with color stock and any special lighting.

Set Decorum

To the uninitiated, a film set can be a rather bewildering place, so this following information may help explain all the activity and most importantly what is expected of you.

CREW & CAST: As a crew member you will be expected to listen and heed the staff of harried Assistant Directors. On set, the 1st A.D. is in charge of everything from the time the director calls Cut until he calls Action! On Actors: Do not approach an actor when they are standing alone. They are working, preparing for the upcoming scene and really don't want to be disturbed.

The Call!: As a "take" approaches the 1st A.D. will call for everyone to SETTLE! That means that all unnecessary movement must cease and you should find yourself a comfortable place – careful to be out of the Actor's eyelines – to stand, sit or squat. This is a cue that all talk and even whispering should stop. This will go out by walkie-talkie to all areas of the location/studio and everyone everywhere should act accordingly. If you are "on set" make sure that you are still for the entire duration of the take, without having to move, rise or even shift weight. (Sometimes this will cause the floor to creak or groan and ruin the take). The A.D. should never have to call settle twice! Next, the A.D. will call "CAMERA READY?" and will receive an echo response of "CAMERA READY" if there are no problems, and if there are any issues the Camera Department will indicate the source of the delay. Based on this the A.D. will decide whether or not to stand down or continue ahead. The process is repeated with the Sound. "Sound ready?"

Next, the A.D. calls "ROLL CAMERA" and is answered, "Camera Rolling or Camera Speed." Remember, it takes a second for the camera and sound to reach the proper speed.

Then the call is repeated for Sound. Next, the Director calls the all-important "Action" and a moment later or a "beat" later the actor or action begins. And when the "take" is finished, the Director will call "CUT" which the A.D. will repeat to the rest of the crew through the walkie-talkie. Note: the only other people who should cut a scene are the camera and soundman ONLY if there is a technical problem. An actor should not "cut" the scene themselves but continue through the take until the end. Unless of course, something very serious is happening like it might be a matter of personal safety or something. However, outside of that exception, an actor should never make the Director have to cut the scene. The reason for this is that there might be something worth keeping in the take.

FOR CAST: Getting into trouble on a film/T.V. set, is extremely easy. Remember, the crew member, for the most part, have been working days, weeks, even months on the production and you must be respectful of them.

I have provided the following list of the various departments and their Do's and Don'ts.

A.D. Department: BE ON TIME! To avoid this – be early. ALWAYS INFORM AN A.D. WHEN LEAVING SET. If the 1st AD is busy, then find one of his staff and tell them. Never assume that if you tell another crew member that the message will be given to the proper person. When leaving for the day ask for a call sheet for the next day's shooting (if you are scheduled)

Wardrobe Department: Never take a piece of your wardrobe home. This includes anything of your own that is in the film. At lunch always be very careful. Sometimes this means that you will be eating wearing a bib or makeup shirt on.

Makeup/hair Department: Be careful at lunch not to spill food or drink on yourself. During down time, do not do anything that causes you to sweat unnecessarily.

Props/art dept/gun handlers: NEVER TAKE ANYTHING FROM THE SET UNLESS ASKED TO. WHEN HANDLING GUNS ALWAYS ASSUME THAT THEY ARE LOADED. This way you give them the respect they deserve.

Chapter Three

Working Into The Script

Navigating into the core of the script or scene requires know-how. The following pages are from my own personal work notes that I would use to guide my actors through my fulltime programs. They are a wealth of knowledge and exercises. Read them, study them, and work with them, for they will take you deeper into the understanding of being an actor, a character, a performance and all that comes with it.

I will start will some thoughts about "acting on film: from some very distinguished people.

"The actor must be prepared to create a role and know that as soon as it is filmed, their performance will never change. The usual procedure is to shoot as many takes of the scene as needed. Then, the director decides to move on. But once that decision is made, there's no turning back. To redo a scene days or weeks later is rare, and is more often caused by the film being damaged at the lab than by a director wishing to reshoot. This means one thing to the actor: YOU HAVE ONE CHANCE TO GET IT RIGHT." (Ian Bernard)

"We all know you can do a lot without saying anything...in behavior...you can do more with one eyebrow sometimes, then with ten lines of dialogue. If you can do it with a look, it might be better." (Robert De Niro)

"The reaction sheet is one of the most important elements of film acting...Since the actor doesn't know prior to shooting when these reaction shots may happen, he must prepare in a general way. It is then that the subtitles of film acting come into play...the reaction shot, to be effective, depends wholly on the ability of the actor to listen!" (Ian Bernard)

"It's fatal to act in film. Listening is the most important thing. Think about what is being said. (Rex Harrison)

"For the involved actor – reacting is the direct result of listening. Unfortunately, the clever actor can listen intellectually and remain uninvolved emotionally. The fact is that listening, real listening (though difficult enough to master) is safe. Reacting is not. You can listen technically, but reacting demands involvement and you must gain the freedom to allow the other actor to act upon you." (Ian Bernard & Ms. Mathieu-Byers)

"Learning your technical blocking and not varying from it is a must. A good actor will use the marking time to your their homework. You can measure the number of steps it takes to get to the door. You can make a note always to turn the same way on each take. Most important, you can assure the technical people that you will give them no surprises when it comes time to shoot. Technical mistakes can rob an actor of precious energy. The technical details of blocking must become automatic so you can attack performance with a clear mind. Make sure your body, hands, and feet are all connected to your brain." (Ian Bernard & Ms. Mathieu-Byers)

"During your preparation, you should make notes of what you want to do and where you want to do it. You should be prepared to defend your deeds with irrefutable dramatic logic. You must also differentiate between blocking moves and pieces of business. Blocking moves, for the most part, fulfill the requirements of the director. Blocking is the choreography that allows creative choices in the editing process. Pieces of business, on the other hand, are the small extras that can make an extraordinary effective characterization." (Ian Bernard)

"An actor in a play, when he gets up in the morning, knows that at eight o'clock that night, he will perform. His whole day is geared to that fact. The actor in a film has no idea when he will be called upon to do a scene. After the call, it could be 10 minutes, or it could be 5 hours. Then, an assistant comes, and there you are in front of the camera, and you have to do it!" (Glenn Jordan)

"You have to know how to talk to actors. Directors who don't, talk to them about feeling, but directors who do, will talk to them about doing. You don't ever say to an actor, "Get mad at

Chapter Three

this guy." What you might say is, "You let that person know, if he tries this again, you're going to murder him. And make damn sure that you see it in his eyes, and he understands how serious you are." Because that's a "Do-able" thing." (Sydney Pollack)

"Let the script speak for itself. Put your character into that world. Don't try to enhance it. Just live in it. With your solid preparation, your character exists truthfully, no matter how unreal some of the situations may be." (Ian Bernard)

"The director approached a scene with the whole film in mind. It is our job to see how this scene fits into the mosaic. The director is the only person who knows what effect the whole film will have on an audience. At least, theoretically we hope that's so. The actor is saying, "Wait a minute, I wouldn't do that. Why would I do that?" that's when I have to say, "You do that because, don't you remember on Page 4, that such and such happened. And we haven't shot that yet. Let's go back and read the pages that affect this scene." You should constantly go back and do your homework while they're setting up, so you know where you're going to be emotionally. Sometimes actors don't do that. They play each scene separately. That's why directors and actors have to have a very close relationship – a little bit closer than it is in the theatre." (Norman Jewison)

"Good technique frees the artist to create. A lot of people have said this, but still, some students of acting resist. Today's films and television industry is sophisticated, knowledgeable and cautious. The well-prepared actor has a much better chance of building a career than the seat-of-the-pants talent...Memorizing the part, knowing lines and business and blocking are certainly part of preparation. But you must be careful that these very important ingredients don't take over. A more comprehensive description of preparation would be this. You know what the character ants every single moment and have a rationale for each action. You have already experienced similar conditions in workshops, classes, exercises, and self-study, so when you are actually cast in a part, you are familiar with the problems. Too many actors prepare only after they are cast in a part. The smart actor prepares each day for that eventuality." (Ian Bernard)

"You have to make choices, no director in the world can help you with that. They can reject what they don't like, but they're your choices. You're using your craft eventually, but all the craft in the world won't help you make choices." (Gene Hackman)

"The critics are apt to say, "The actor hadn't found the character." The comment is usually caused by the actor looking for the character during performance. What the audience sees is a series of interesting vignettes, a schizophrenic rambling when the actor fails to achieve a coherent persona. Relying on the gods or the muses to find character almost always results in a performance where the character changes from scene to scene." (Ian Bernard)

"Emotional Preparation" means an undistracted, centered and open to whatever happens in the scene actor – it DOES NOT mean that you have to "do" something to create an emotional state in yourself." (Ms. Mathieu-Byers)

Diane Ackerman wrote in an article in the New York Times: "There is a code of basic facial expressions that all humans share – happiness, anger, fear, surprise, disgust. Spontaneous, automatic, the face forms words before the mind can think of them. We often rely on facial semaphore to tell us truths too subtle or shameful or awkward or intimate or emotionally charged or nameless to speak."

"The face forms words before the mind can think them." Very provocative! It suggests that we react first on a primal level, then think. The actor must be that prepared, and that focused, and that open and relaxed in order to allow themselves to react that organically. It will get caught In the close-up!" (Ian Bernard & Ms. Mathieu-Byers)

"I think the most boring thing in the world is to play results. If you play the laugh rather than the character, it never is funny." (Louise Latham)

Chapter Three

"The key to comedy acting is credibility. You must think that you as the character are funny." (Ian Bernard)

"The problem with comedy scenes in playback is that after you've viewed the second or third version, the reactions begin to fizzle. Thee something happens on the set as you perform the scene a dozen times. By the twelfth time, the edge is gone, and you panic. This usually triggers a dangerous response, from the actor – he makes radical changes in choices, new, broader business. Mugging, Ad lobbing, Playing to the camera instead of the other actor, ALL DEADLY." (Ian Bernard)

"In situation comedy, continuing characters do a book show: that is, show with a story line. Because situations are a major source of employment, it's a good idea to examine how they work from the actor's point of view. If there is one word to describe the difference between acting for situation comedy and acting for film and television comedy in long form (movies, teleplays), I nominate "exaggeration when playing comedy; I suggested giving an edge to the character. In sitcom, you can give it two edges and not be afraid of going over. Every sitcom character is a bit of a caricature." (Ian Bernard)

First reading of the script

Remember, the actor is a storyteller. You paint a picture in the minds of the viewer with each word you speak or gesture you make or each reaction you show no matter how slight.

To be a good storyteller mean you need to know and understand every detail in the story you are telling. Professionals in the acting industry know all too well that if there is going to be a problem in the film, then you will find that problem in the script first. Its essential know how to visualize what the writer is saying in your mind's eye when reading the script and "learn to know" what works and what won't work from script to film.

The following pages will help you understand how to get a better understanding of the inner workings of the script that you can use again and again in all your works to come.

So first up is what's called the "script structure." The vast majority of the work you will do is known as the traditional Three Act Structure. I think it obvious to say that since the dawn of man telling stories that each and every story has a Beginning, a Middle and an End.

Its laid out like this:

ACT ONE – Beginning (known as the setup / Introduction of the characters - Hero, Villains and who wants what.)

ACT TWO – Middle (The confrontation between Hero and Villain)

ACT THREE - End (The resolution. Hero wins. Villain loses)

Television scripts follow the same Three Act Structure, however, unlike feature films, TV shows have commercial breaks, and as such, they are divided into "Act Breaks."

Chapter Three

Here then is a typical TV script structure:

> Half-Hour Episodic TV (22-25 pages
>
> One-Hour Episodic TV (50-65 pages
>
> Two Hour TV Movie (100-110 pages

A TV script can be further broken down when seeing that most TV shows use a Teaser and a Tag. For example, your typical one-hour TV show would layout like this below:

> **Teaser:** 2-4 pages
> **Act One:** 14-15 pages
> **Act Two:** 14-15 Pages
> **Act Three:** 14-15 Pages
> **Act Four:** 14-15 Pages
> **Tag:** 1-2 Pages
> **Total:** 59 to 66 pages

Okay, now you know how story structured fits into films and Television shows. So now, when you first settle down to reading your script or scene for the first time make sure to be in a relaxing space where you will be not interrupted as you ready the start from beginning to the end.

Your first reading should be to get what the story is about. Who are the characters and what each wants and why? It's this first read that will tell you if the story is exciting or boring. Was it fun or tedious to read? (Remember that reading a screenplay is not the same as reading a novel. More on that later)

The Actors Success In The Making

Okay now, this time you are going to read the script again and this time have a pencil and notepaper handy. This time when you read it you are going to make note of the following:

- What was the story about? In story terms, the story is known as the PLOT?
- What is the main action that hooks the audience?
- What does the Villain (ANTAGONIST) want and why does he or she want it?
- What does the Hero (PROTAGONIST) want and what does he or she want it?
- What are both the Hero and the Villain clashing over?
- What central problem has been created and how is it to be solved?
- What happens to the main characters?
- What are the characters doing and thinking?
- What are the main dramatic issues in the story?
- What is the ending or conclusion to the story?)
- Who is the most interesting character and why?
- Where does the story take place including time period?
- What is the "message" behind the story or THEME? Most good scripts have a central message that they want the reader to walk away with. For example, in the movie *Scarface*, the message for the viewer is that, no matter how big and powerful you are, crime doesn't pay.
- Does the story go from a sense of or real "slavery" to a sense of or real freedom? If so how?

Chapter Three

Screenplay Format

Standard screenplay format contains the following elements:

1. Each scene begins with a full-page-width capitalized scene heading that list:

- Number of scene (once all rewrites are complete)
- Interior or exterior
- Location
- Main characters involved
- Time of the day or night

2. Body copy (action description, mood setting, and stage directions) is double-spaced away from the scene headings dialogue and runs the width of the page.

3. All character names outside dialogue are capitalized.

4. Dialogue sections are:

- Within narrow margins
- Preceded and followed by a double space
- Headed by the speaker's name in capitals and centered, and
- Accompanied when strictly necessary by stage directions inside brackets

5. Shot transitions like "Cut to," "Dissolve to," etc., used only when strictly necessary, placed either flush left or flush right.

On the next page is an example of screenplay format: From A NIGHT SO LONG by Lynise Pion)

14. INT.   LIBRARY CAFETERIA – NOON – DANA & ED

DANA places a mug of coffee on her tray nest to her red helmet. She slides the array in sync with the quick pace of the line crowded with impatient students. She stops at the heat lamp glowing over several small cartoons of French fries. She picks up a carton and contemplates the soggy, yellow potatoes. DANA sighs and places the fries on her tray.

ED's VOICE

You can't live on French fries alone.

DANA, started, turns to ED who is chomping a huge banana.

DANA

Do you always sneak up on people?

ED moves along side DANA as she progresses to the grill.

ED

You were up and out early...

DANA reads the menu above the grill.

DANA

I've got classes, remember?

ED

Try the Varsity Burger, it's not bad.

DANA

Whose lunch is this?

ED touches DANA on the arm with his banana hand.

DANA glares at the menu.

Chapter Three

Screenplay Analysis

On the pervious page, there was an example of a screenplay with no camera or editing direction. Industry practice varies; many commercial scripts try to dramatize their contents by breaking each scene into shots and making it closer to a shooting script.

ACTORS TAKE NOTE: The screenplay format tends to reinforce the impression that films are built theatrically around dialogue. Good screen drama is primarily about behavior. Remember, <u>what you say</u> is not as important as <u>how you say it</u>, and <u>how you say it</u> is based on <u>how you feel</u>, and <u>how you feel</u> is based on <u>what's happening in the scene</u>. Films are NOT radio dramas.

Good Screenplay Essentials

Good screenplay essentials to know is that there do not include the author's thoughts, instructions, or comments.

Does not leave most of the behavior to the reader's imagination. It may describe the effect "economically" but NOT as a novel might take a whole sentence or even half a page to get the same meaning out to the reader. Example: "She looks angry, walks to the door and slams it shut behind her," instead of: "She grits her teeth in silence, then walks calmly towards the open door; fully aware that she is being watched. She stands for a moment in the archway. Stiffens her backbone in defiance. Then with her withered hand, she gently, almost with a spider's delicacy, wraps her bony fingers around the polished, brass, door handle. Then she slams the heavy oak door shut with an almighty bang!

Film Dialogue

The dialogue used in films is not the same as dialogue used in real life. The dialogue in movies is written to allow for what the camera makes clear for the telling of the story. In movies, each character has their own dialogue characteristics, and vocabulary. However, in real life, people communicate elliptically, meaning without sufficient transition or a logical connection between thoughts, ideas, or expressions. In movies, the dialogue carries the story, the plot. Each line of dialogue must carry the story along to the films end.

Preparing To Interpret The Text

FIRST IMPRESSIONS. The first time reading through a screenplay, read it quickly, without interruption, noting your random first impressions. These can be vital resources later when essentials become blurred through over-familiarity with detail.

First impressions are intuitive and become more significant with greater familiarity. When finished, read it again and then examine the impressions the story left on you.

• What did it make you feel?

• Who did you care about?

• Who did you find interesting?

• What is the screenplay really dealing with under the surface events?

Note down these impressions and read the screenplay once or twice again looking for evidence of what you picked up.

Next ask: What is the important message I take away from the screenplay? What's the bigger story the screenplay is trying to get out, (if any?) Make note of these thoughts.

Next, go through the screenplay again and make a list of the scenes, giving each a one or two sentences of description. This method will provide you a much clearer idea of the intended film's dramatic logic. Also, when reading the screenplay, you want to study the BACKSTORY, which are the

Chapter Three

events in the story that have brought the characters to the script's present.

Also, you want to find YOUR CHARACTER'S GIVEN CIRCUMSTANCES. Meaning, know at every point what circumstances, time, place, pressures, and other people are contributing to your character's physical and mental state.

Next, begin to put together a BIOGRAPHY of your character. Make up (imagine if you have too) a full life story for your character, one that supports the backstory details implied by in the script. This method will help you get a more intuitive feeling of the character and that everything your character says or does is rooted in the patterns of behavior created by his or her past. Without this backstory, your character will lack true experiences and motivations that have shaped him or her. Your character will lack depth and credibility but will just be a superficial character. It's important to note that sometimes the director will ask you questions during rehearsal about your character's background and having a clear knowledge of your characters past will help you help the director bring out the true layers of your character.

Also, you want to be able to JUSTIFY EVERYTHING YOUR CHARACTER SAYS AND DOES. It is so important for you to know the pressures motivating your character's every action and every line. You find this out by reading each of your character's lines and ask yourself, what is my character's objective in saying this or doing this. What's making my character do this?

You have already used this process of "justification" when you created your character's biography, and remember, it's this biography which rules your character's choices and decisions.

Next, you want to DEFINE EACH ACTION WITH AN ACTIVE VERB. Meaning, to change a verb from the passive to the active voice, or to make the subject of the passive verb the object of the active verb. The person or thing performing the action becomes the subject of the new sentence.

Like in real life, it's not what you say that really matters it's what actions you do. Well, this is the same for movies. In fact, the actions your characters take are of critical importance in telling what's happening for your characters and in the story.

When you define each of your characters actions with an "active Verb," you are serving to clarify the behavior of your character and her or her motivation behind the action. Every action taken by your character MUST have a true to life motivation. For example, if your characters were to scratch his or her head for a moment. If you do the action without motivation this is not true to life. A true to life motivation might by that you scratched your head because your scalp was itchy at that moment. Isn't that true to life? Another example might be that you scratched your head because you were trying to solve a confusing problem like, who killed the butler, with what weapon, in what room.

Another really important question to ask of your character is: WHAT IS MY CHARACTER TRYING TO GET?

Answering this question is the lynchpin of your character and is the key to your acting, because if you don't know your characters objective then how can you act out what he or she is doing? You can't; your actions lack true direction to an objective. It's like getting into a car, starting up the engine, and just sitting there not knowing where to go. Now, if on the other hand, you do have an OBJECTIVE, then your next choice is how to get there. This choice depends on what's happening to your character in the moment, or what has brought you to this moment. For example, let's look at the actions of a little kid in the supermarket with her mother. The kid wants a little chocolate egg. The kid, very nicely, asks for the egg, but the mother, very nicely says "not today honey, you've had enough chocolate." Okay, so now the battle lines are drawn, because the kid does want the egg, and the kid intends to get the egg.

Chapter Three

SCENE PLAYS OUT:

KID
I want the egg, Mommy.

MOTHER
Not now honey, I told you.

KID (cries)
Mommy, I want the egg!!

MOTHER
Please, now I said no, and I mean no.

KID (screams)
I want my egg! You're so mean!! My egg!!!

Everyone in the store looks at the "evil" mother denying her lovely child from having one little egg. KID CRIES LOUDER. MOTHER takes the egg and hands it to the kid. Kid stops screaming.

KID (smiles)
I love you, Mommy.

END OF SCENE.

So, you can see that the kid worked all the choices she had in her little toolbox. She worked the mother into the situation where the mother felt she had no choice but to give in, and she did. In conclusion: the kid had an objective and tried many ways to get what she wanted. That's true to life for people. We have objectives, and we try many ways to get what we want. The same holds true for your character. So, find the objective and see how many ways you try to get what you want using the text as is written in the scene. You can also use actions or expressions.

Another thing to make note of when reading your screenplay is: WHAT ARE THE OTHER CHARACTERS TRYING TO DO TO ME OR GET FROM ME? This is super important because knowing the answer is was causes the conflict in a story, or in the scene. Remember, CONFLICT drives your story.

Now in real life, people's desires wants, needs and intentions shift from moment to moment depending on the situation. People are in a constant state of being spontaneous, always shifting from taking on roles of either being defensive or offensive. These roles that your character plays out, moment to moment are dictated by your characters ever-shifting situations. If you play this type of reality in your work, then your character is living truthfully from one moment to the next, just like in real life.

On the next couple of pages, I have provided two blueprints of establishing and clarifying your characters situations. The first is the Basic 6 W'S and the second is the C.R.O.W.S.

The Basic 6 W'S

WHO AM I? This is your character.

- What do other characters say about your character?
- What does your character say about himself/herself?

WHAT TIME IS IT?

- Century, Year, Season, Month, Day, Hour, Minute

WHERE AM I?

- Country, City, Neighborhood, House, Room, Area of the room
- Indoors? Outdoors?

WHAT DO I WANT?

- Character's psychological motivation

Chapter Three

WHAT IS IN MY WAY OF GETTING WHAT I WANT?

- Character's obstacles

WHAT DO I DO TO GET WHAT I WANT?

- Character's ACTION – both physical & verbal obstacles

C.R.O.W.S

When reading your screenplay apply the C.R.O.W.S as follows:

C: Character: Refers to the character they are portraying. Read the screenplay or the scenes and make a list of your characters characteristics, example: physicality, speech patterns, mannerisms, dialects, etc.

R: Relationship: Find the SPECIFIC details of your relationship with the person whom you are speaking to in your scene or commercial.

O: Objective: This is stated in one sentence. The objective is what you want from the other person. It should be in the form of a statement. "I want you to........." This is an action word (verb), not a predetermined emotion state or description of what you think is going in the scene.

W: Where: This again is SPECIFIC in its description. If you are in a house, whose house? What room? Are you alone or around other people? What does the room have in it? Again you must "see" and sense the DETAILS!

S: Situation: Another explanation for this is the GIVEN CIRCUMSTANCES. It is the circumstances that lead up to the scene, i.e. the history of the characters, what was said before the first line of the scene, what is the emotional state at the beginning of the scene.

Scene Analysis

Okay then, now that you have drilled down into the overall story, it's time to drill down and analyze each scene throughout your script, even the scenes you are not playing a role in. So read your scene and then answer these questions

- What is the scene about?
- How does the scene drive the story forward?
- What is the climax or high point of the scene?
- What has been resolved in this scene?
- How does the scene end?
- What do you feel were the important lines spoken that moved the story forward?
- Were there any lines, words, or actions in the scene that you fell a personal connection to? What were they and why?
- Which character drove the story forward?
- What were the emotional highs and lows in the scene?

The term "BEAT" in a script or screenplay has two meanings:

1/ is where the actor pauses his words or actions and its an opportunity to have a mental thought to be picked up by the camera/audience. The director may say to you "take a beat on that word, or before you do that or that."

2 / "Beat" can also mean sections within the scene where there is a change in the objective, action, or emotion, or purpose, then that is called a beat-change. So in the light of that explanation, you would answer this question:

- What was the "Beat-changes" that moved the story forward?

Chapter Three

In-Depth Scene Analysis & Character Study Process

1. Read the scene or script without making early "acting" or "character" judgments

2. Ask what's the objective of your character?

3. Apply C.R.O.W.S and THE BASIC 6 W'S

4. Write down everything about your character that you can think of as to who your character is and get this impression/information from what you have read. Include anything that other characters mention about your character, also pay attention to any actions that your character does because actions reveal a lot.

5. What are the other characters trying to do to me or get from me?

6. BACK-STORY. Write out and know the events that brought the characters to the script's present. Know at every point what circumstances, time, place, pressures, and other people are contributing to your character's physical and mental state.

7. BIOGRAPHY / Make up a full life story for your character, one that supports the backstory details implied by the script. This ensures that you know a great deal about the character you are creating and that everything your character says or does is rooted in the patterns created by his or her past. Without this integrity of experience and motivation, your character will lack depth and credibility. The director will often question you during rehearsal about your character's background, always centering on those aspects that are not coming across well. **And make sure you hand write it all out — this ways it gets into your body.**

8. Write out all your lines in ONE SENTENCE with NO grammar or punctuation

9. Highlight in one color any words or phrases (from your one sentence) that have a personal connection or resonate with you on a personal note.

10. Highlight in a different color any words or phrases that YOU BELIEVE are important to your character. Be clear on this. Not every word is important and means something to your character, so read thoroughly and ***know why those words are important to your character***

11. Learn the lines from this one sentence FIRST. Work them into your mental system

12. Write out what you are really saying behind the words you are saying

13. Then take all that you have discovered back over to your actual scene or script pages, adding the highlights and any special notes you have included

14. Apply "Emotions" on the left side of page and "Objectives" on the right side of the page AND start both at the top of the page and work your way through the material. Know what your emotion is before you say the line and know the objective as to why you are saying that line. And work your way through all your lines. ***Remember, it's not so important about what you say but HOW you say it. And how you say it is based upon how you FEEL and how you feel is based upon what you THINK (as in "thoughts in your head) and what you think in that moment is based upon what the OTHER ACTOR IS SAYING OR DOING in that moment within that scene. It's all connected, and so you should have a clear understanding of the dynamics that are all related.***

Chapter Three

15. Find the "BEATS" in the scene and identify each "BEAT" And then play each beat when you get to it.

16. Know your MOTIVATING DESIRE <u>(also known as the "character's super objective")</u>. Just as a script has a main idea, every character has some basic, main purpose for being a part of the circumstances of the story. The character's main purpose, the controlling action, reflects the character's most important strivings and should be paramount in determining everything the character says and does — the desire that controls and unifies all the characters actions. *MOTIVATING DESIRE is the single overriding action that all the character's individual actions serve. Once discovered – name it!!! Know it!!! Let it be what's inside you pushing you forward!!!*

17. Now, learn the others persons words but DO NOT MEMORIZE THEM because your work may become stale. **Know your lines 100% but only have an idea of the others person lines.** This will help keep the freshness edge. Remember once all this work is done you are meant to "let it go" and just forget it like it never happened. And when the director say's "action" you begin the scene as if you have never heard it before, listening for the **first time for real, allowing your reactions to be honest,** and keep the freshness.

18. ***ALWAYS LOOK TO RAISE THE STAKES!**** Read your scene and try to feel where the beats are in the scene for you as the actor / your character can organically raise your **emotional investment** into the situation happening now in that scene/moment. <u>***AND KEEP YOUR PERFORMANCE REAL!!***</u>

WHY READING SCREENPLAYS MAY BE DIFFICULT

Screenplays are not like novels. If you have never read a screenplay before you are going to find it very different. A screenplay is like a blueprint of something yet to be crafted, being the movie. A screenplay consists of dialogue, some stage directions and some remarks on each character as they appear, as well as location and behavior. The screenplay is a verbal map consisting of impressions of what the film should be like.

16 Steps To Creating Your Character

1. Enter into the scene and the characters within like an explorer on a quest of discovery.

2. Discover the relationship between your character and the other character.

3. Find your objective – your desire – what you are fighting for

4. Find the conflict and fight for it.

5. Think about the moment before the scene began.

6. Look for the humor.

7. Find the opposites of how to play a moment in a scene.

8. Find what is of true Importance to your character in this scene.

9. Find the events in this scene that stand out.

10. What and where is the "place" in which this scene is taking place?

11. Try role-playing out your character through improvisation.

12. Are you in competition with the other person or something else?

13. Discover the mystery or secret of your character or within the scene by asking yourself, "What's really going on with my character or in this scene."

14. Read between the lines of what is being spoken between the characters. What are they and YOU really saying?

15. What would you love to say to the other person?

16. What's the "internal conflict" going on inside of you? Meaning, is your character worried about something? Are you holding yourself back for some reason?

3 Questions To Ask As Your Character

As your CHARACTER, answer these questions:

1. What gets you out of bed every morning and injects you into your daily life?

2. What drives you?

3. Paint a written picture of your own deeper wish. After you have done this, sum up your desires into a simple, specific and short "phrase." This phrase is you as the character. It's your core.

Next: Who am I? (as your character) This is the question that has been asked by scholars for thousands of years. Simply take a pad of paper and write one sentence describing who you are and keep adding to the list. This process will help you tune into your character quicker. Also, be aware that the answers you provide above are also the parts that affect your characters behavior, actions and thoughts.

Everything your character will do, say and think is ruled by what your character believes about themselves. So, what does your character believe?

Super Objective, Through-Line & Obligatory Actions/Events

The play or screen play's main idea is the intention that the writer wanted to accomplish when he or she wrote the script. It is the essence or philosophical core of the play. Everything done by the director, actors, designers, etc. must be in service to the SUPER OBJECTIVE that everyone understands. (Sometimes an actor can experiment with many choices for actions. The choices may be based on the actor's intuitive impulses, talents, habits, and ideas. The bottom line here is, if the actors and even the director don't take into account the SUPER OBJECTIVE, they end up telling personal stories at the expense of the writer.)

You may not be able to determine the author's intention solely from a first read through of the screenplay. The same basic story may be used to express a variety of intentions, and you are going to have to do multiple reads to peel back the layers and look below the surface of the text to see how the plot expresses observations about human behavior, society, or world events. Or you may have to go the metaphorical – in any case – to determine the SUPER OBJECTIVE may take a careful examination.

Also be aware – that the DIRECTOR can decide what the SUPER OBJECTIVE is regardless of what the writer thinks. Make sure you know what the director thinks the philosophical point is – that is the point you cannot violate.

Chapter Three

How To Choose A Super Objective

1. Make the Big List

Go through the screenplay and write down all the non-interpretive actions – everything that the character decides to do both leading up to and during the events of the story. Try to be as objective about the facts possible. Make notes to indicate which facts are reported and believed to be true but not proven by the audience actually seeing it happen.

2. Make the Short List

Go through the list and put a star by the ones that seem to be especially significant. The starred items are not just what the playwright seems to think are central. More important are those things that you personally have the most trouble understanding yourself choosing to do. To clean up the list, write the starred items all over again in one place as a Short List.

3. Pick a Trial Super Objective

Write down a super objective – a single sentence that states what you are trying to get from someone else that would make you chose to do all the things on the Short List.

4. Test the Trial Super Objective

Does it serve the screenplay? Go through all the items on the Big List and make sure you can explain how everything, even the most trivial choices, are part of the character's attempt to get the Trial Super-Objective.

5. Commit Yourself to the Super Objective

Don't keep questioning it. Don't keep worrying about it. You have chosen it. You have tested it. It is yours to use – and to enjoy using.

Some tips on #3: Remember, express objectives as long as they state what you want someone else to do. Is there an action you want them to perform (hug me, kiss my butt). Is there a role you want them to play in your life (be my slave, be my guru)? If you can't figure out what you want others to do, state what you want for yourself and then figure out how others could be a part of helping you to get it.

Motivating Desire

The motivation desire, (also known as the "character's super objective") is the backbone of every character and has some basic, main purpose for being a part of the circumstances of the play. The character's main purpose, the controlling action, reflects the character's most important strivings and should be paramount in determining everything the character says and does — the desire that controls and unifies all the characters actions.

MOTIVATING DESIRE is the single overriding action that all the character's individual actions serve. Once discovered – name it!!! A character's MOTIVATING DESIRE must be in harmony with the script's SUPER OBJECTIVE – it may not violate the print of the SUPER OBJECTIVE.

Through – Line Of Action

A logical, consecutive series of a character's actions based on and in harmony with a character's motivating desire. A character's THROUGH-LINE flows from one action to the next throughout the course of the play. Since it forms an unbroken line from scene to scene (a beat to beat), it serves to keep the actor on track and working towards a definite accomplishable goal.

The THROUGH-LINE harmonizes with the MOTIVATING DESIRE which is itself in harmony with the author's SUPER OBJECTIVE for the play (screenplay) as a whole.

Chapter Three

The THROUGH-LINE (Spine) controls the logic of the character's actions and makes the theme of the script concrete – uniting the character into a seamless whole. The THROUGH-LINE prevents the actor from being distracted by secondary or unimportant events – it becomes the organic tie that unites all the character's parts into one piece. It is an overall plan for the actions of your character.

CHANGES

Events make a films progress. That event can be a CHANGE. These changes can be overt or covert – obvious or concealed – merely subtle or outright obscure. Whatever form of the changes, their effects will be felt later on as plot advances. Since CHANGES can be strong events, actors must keep a sharp lookout for CHANGES in their characters.

CONFRONTATION

Events in the screenplay can be CONFRONTATIONS because every CONFRONTATION achieves some result and makes some change in relationships or in the story. Things are never the same after a CONFRONTATION.

PSYCHOLOGICAL

Major actions are often found in discoveries one character makes about another character. That "Ah-ha!" moment when a character is finally able to perceive the deeper truth of a situation or a character, can be a wonderful moment. Nothing can ever be the same after such a discovery. A character begins the act of discovery by taking small steps. First, the character realizes something is not right and then as the character's awareness heightens, several of these small discoveries lead to one large one that changes everything.

STORY CLIMAX

CLIMAXES are turning points in the lives of the characters, out of which the stakes of the story are heightened, or the plot turns in a new direction. CLIMAXES typically close off some avenues while opening others. CLIMAX in the classic sense –

is a single event play, however, in movies, there is more than one CLIMAX per act. In TV they are built-in just in time for commercial breaks.

Bottom line is this: It is the actor's job to find at least one major action and/or event in every scene

Notes On Performing For Film

Making films is a technical process first! Remember to allow 90% of you to get into the scene but keep 10% of your mind grounded in the work reality. It's this 10 percent that keeps you and the other actors safe and keeps you in the camera frame. This also keeps the director happy because if the camera can't see it, then it's lost to the viewer.

Also, make sure you have "thoughts" running in your head as your character. What are your characters "thoughts' at any given moment in a scene? Know this because "thoughts" read on camera, meaning that the camera can see you thinking. So you have to "think" like the character. Don't forget this.

Listening & Reading!

The true listener learns that if he or she trusts to listening, freshly, as for the first time, each time, then he or she will perceive things that they would not otherwise perceive, and will begin to feel.

SIMPLICITY! Simplicity demands that you trust yourself. If you are genuinely listening to the other character, you would be using **all your senses & responsive to stimuli**. If that be true, then you would not be lacking in an emotion or verbal or physical expression/response/articulation. Your responses would be real. You don't have to push; you don't have to indicate, or illustrate, or ACT it out for us. It will be there, and it will be the truth.

Chapter Three

VOCALLY: There is no artifice or determined pacing in the dialogue. Vocal pacing comes in the editing process. So space your words as the thoughts dictate and you'll be good.

PHYSICALLY: If the camera does not see your acting, then the audience will not see it. So, remember to take the camera with you.

Try to apply as much of all the above as possible, where possible. It's easier if you are on the project from the start but if you are a day players then do the best you can. The day players have a harder job of it because you have to show up on a day – lines learned, character created, homework & research done, and be ready to shoot – often without benefit of rehearsal, without meeting the other cast members, without ever seeing the environment and sometimes without ever having had the chance to meet and/or discuss the role with the director. I know being a day player is hard, but we all have gone through it, and so prepare as much as you can, be fellable and have fun.

CHAPTER FOUR
The Winner's Circle

Overall Success Strategies

Always read aloud your lines over and over about 30 times, and then write them down to get them into your body where possible and say your lines as you walk through your "blocking" to get it naturally in your body.

It's a great idea to do student, low-budget, and independent films. Do community and independent theater and gain performance experience. Try a variety of roles. This will allow you to stretch and become a better-rounded actor. It's a great idea to look-up acting jobs every day. Try these sites: Playbill, Mandy.com, Backstage, Actors Access, Acting Magazine, and Craigslist. Try joining a theater group or company or begin your own. Pick a monologue that says something reflective of who you are and what you believe.

Remember, when going to see an agent, walk into the office smiling, and create an atmosphere where you can both get to know each other as people. Don't try to sell yourself; everyone does that. Instead, try to have a conversation about how beautiful the day is or something interesting you have seen in their office, or how about a great movie you just saw?

Always have at least two monologues, drama, and comedy that are all 100% memorized and ready to go.

Always choose an age-appropriate monologue about 1 ½ minutes in length.

If you are doing a Shakespeare piece make sure you know EXACTLY what you're saying. Get a dictionary, and a Shakespeare Lexicon, that is a reference book defining every word Shakespeare uses.

Chapter Four

Remember to learn to "paraphrase" the monologue in your own modern-day words/language. This will help you get a clearer understanding and feeling of what you are saying. Then take those feelings and understandings back to the Shakespearean text.

10 Success Strategies For An Actor

1/ YOU NEED TO UNDERSTAND THE INDUSTRY: Read up on the industry, learn from the great actors of the silver screen, and trust me, you have a lot to learn. Purchase a biography book on your favorite actors and learn how they did it. Read books on directors and how some of the great films were made.

2/ BE REALISTIC: Your chances of becoming a "star" are extremely remote. It's like trying to win the lottery, and yes people do win the lottery, and people do become movie stars, but for every jackpot winner or "star" there are millions of hopefuls that don't win anything – not even a set of steak knives. Therefore my advice for you is, don't set yourself up to win a future Oscar, because you will most likely not win one. However, truly take the time to strive and be the best actor or performer you can be, and just let the magic happen. And have fun doing it.

3/ YOU NEED TRAINING: Get training in university, college, a drama program, or acting courses. Get on camera training as well, how to audition for commercials, film and TV audition, etc. There are so many options out there for you to choose from.

4/ YOU NEED DYNAMIC HEADSHOTS: Headshots are your business cards. The headshot is the first time agents, casting or producers will see you, and you want those photos to be the best! Don't rush or go cheap on them, and don't get your best friend to take them either. Get professional shots. That doesn't mean you need to spend thousands of dollars, but be prepared to spend up to $500. Remember, it's more important for you to find a professional photographer that you feel comfortable with, and who can bring out your best personality and charisma for the shot.

5/ YOU NEED TO BE POSITIVE: You have to understand that your energy will affect the people around you. How you feel will determine how and what you do, and your actions will either drain people of their own personal energy, or you can inspire them. No one likes to hang around with someone who complains and gossips and generally has a poor self-esteem. However, people love to be with people who are exciting, friendly, passionate and inspirational. Which type of person are you?

6/ YOU NEED TO BE PROACTIVE: This means you need to be taking action every day towards your career. Each day you should be doing something: like looking in trade papers, casting websites, reading articles of the movies being made so you can audition, reading a stars biography and learn how they did it, looking up a new monologue or taking another class. But here is the truth, most people reading this book will not do anything towards their career and others will only half-heartedly take some form of passive action towards living their dreams. And that's why most people will fail. What about you?

7/ HIGHER PURPOSE: You must have a higher purpose in your life that is beyond your acting career. Ask yourself "why" you want this? What's your real purpose; your real motivation?

8/ BUSINESS ENTREPRENEUR: Think like a business entrepreneur, meaning know your stuff and make decisions and go for it. However, you must think of your financial investment. It's going to cost money to get set-up and going, so make a budget of what's needed to set-up, start your business, and maintain you for a while. You need to get up and get focused, get hungry, get determined, and get some courage to summon up what needs to be done, and get it done every day, like a business or you will FAIL!

Chapter Four

ACTION leads to RESULTS that reinforces your BELIEF that you are either on the right track, or you are not on the right track. If you are on the right track, then your actions/behavior will TAP INTO YOUR POTENTIAL. If you are not on the right track and continue to make no progressive change (as most people do), then you will never know your true potential at anything, and that's tragic.

Look how it works below.

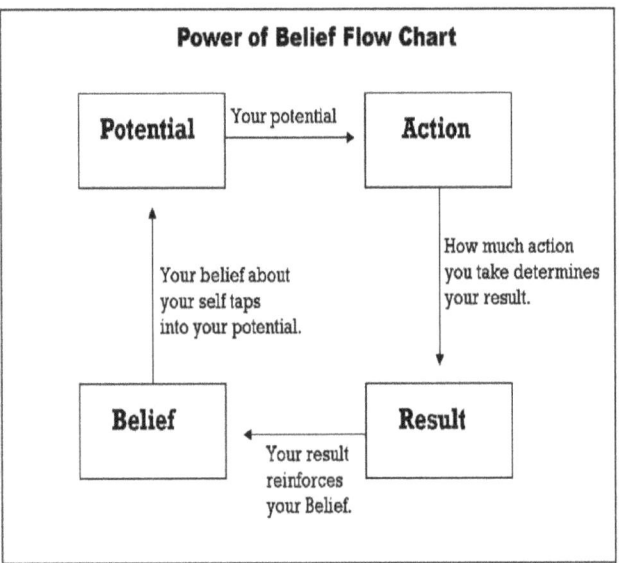

9/ NETWORK: Networking is a vital strategy for your success. You need to make personal connections with other actors, directors, agents, casting directors and producers. Some actors don't like to "schmooze' but you need to learn how to be natural at doing it.

Think of it as getting to know people in the business that you have a mutual respect for. Remember, to build respect you need to be responsible, professional and keep a positive attitude at all times. You need to build a nexus of good people around you, who want to help you be successful, and you can also help them.

10/ NEVER STOP GROWING / NEVER STOP LEARNING. Remember, always be curious about things, look at them like a child would with wonderment. Ask questions, ponder the answers, step up and try it to learn for yourself. Watch movies, watch the 'behind the scenes', go to the theater, learn all you can from who you can. Listen, learn, try it, have fun and stay focused on your dream.

MY PERSONAL MANAGER TIP: I want you today to make a "to do list" regarding your acting career, and begin to take action on completing the points you have made on that list. Then cross off what you have completed, and then add more. Learn to use the list every day, and I promise you, you will begin to move yourself forward with momentum.

Chapter Four

7 ACTION STEPS TO GETTING WORK

Okay so here is the blueprint for getting work as a non-union actor with no agent. First up, you need to take on the agent role and learn to run your own business.

Step 1 / At least get BASIC acting training, or the auditioners will not take you seriously.

Step 2/ Get set-up your own free website. Google free websites and pick the best one for you and then get building. All you need is two pages and then follow the template below.

YOUR NAME	
HEADSHOT	**BIOGRAPHY**
Your actors headshot goes here or create a slideshow of about 3 headshots. One shot is your natural look, one a dramatic look and one a commercial look.	Mention a few words about you, your dreams, who are you? A simple and brief biography that gives the reader an idea about you the person NOT you the actor. Save the actor stuff for your resume
RESUME	**VIDEO**
Your actors resume goes here. Either as a PDF one page download or click the link and it opens to the second page where the resume takes up most of that second page and they just scroll down reading your material.	Your performance reel goes here. Either embed the video into the actual website or upload the video to YouTube and share the video here. Set the video to play automatically when the page is visited.

Remember, when putting your webpage together. Whatever your final page is to look like, make sure it is simple and yet reflects you. Be creative but DO NOT make your page to busy with silly icons and stuff. Keep it professional, simple and welcoming.

Step 3 / Have your professional color headshot ready of you and not your characters. If you only have one shot to put up on your website then ALWAYS make it your personal look, the friendly personality of you and NOT a character. Also, have printed 8x10 copies ready to post if needed to post off in the mail.

Step 4 / Assemble your resume as per the template shown previously.

Step 5 / Here is the tricky one, making the video. If you do have video performances of your work that is NOT shot by mom or dad from way back at the end of the room, then use it. Having said that here is the first rule: the video quality MUST look really good and sound great otherwise don't use it. It does not have to be a Hollywood budget, but it MUST have good video and sound quality.

If you do not have a video of your performances, then you can create them. Create two contrasting scenes, one serious and one light-hearted and create one TV commercial.

The TV commercial should be shot from your mid-chest up and be a stationary camera. Your TV performance energy should be upbeat and conversational. Please do your research on how to best do a TV commercial.

Your acting scenes should be shot in close up, and only you should be in the shot and NOT the off-camera actor. It would be nice if your background somewhat suited your feeling of the scene. Example, if you are doing something serious, then the background will also reflect that mood. However, at the end of the day, it's not the background that is going for the work, it's you. Keep it simple. Keep the camera steady and

Chapter Four

when you say your lines – speak your truth as your character. Do your research on the best way to shoot a scene.

Step 6 / Edit your scenes and TV commercial. Download a (free) editing software or use Microsoft Movie Maker or Sony Vegas Pro. Go to YouTube and learn about editing your videos. You can mix and match your three scenes as you want. For example, you can place the TV commercial between the two scenes. Just put your best work first.

VIDEO EDITING LAYOUT

Below as example is how your finished video should look as laid out on your editing timeline ready to render and export.

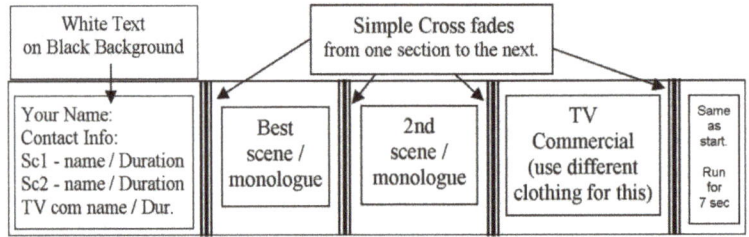

(Note "Dur" means time duration of video)

Below are three photos of how you could play your scenes and TV commercial that work best to favor you as a camera-aware actor.

Photo 1 shows William playing to the right of camera. This angle favors *his* right side of the face.

The Actors Success In The Making

His next scene is played in the opposite direction to the first scene, and this angle then favors his left side of face.

For the TV commercial William then plays to the camera.

By using these angles, the casting people get to see all sides of what your face looks like from any camera angle. It also shows your awareness of how to work with the camera.

Step 7 / Once your two scenes and one commercial have been edited on the one video you are set to now compress your video to a more usable size. Google "Handbrake Software" It's free and it will compress you video size on for your computer to upload better into either the website or onto YouTube. Once you have the Handbrake downloaded and its free by the way, you now need to learn to use it.

Go here on YouTube and learn fast: **Handbrake Tutorial (Best Compression Setting)**
     https://youtu.be/2hmV7g6WTV4

Chapter Four

Now, once you have all you need (resume, photo, and video) set up on your website, now you join the casting websites. **Please do your research** in advance on Google here. One of the best is Mandy.com.

The idea is this: You submit to a casting website, and then you review their site to see what NON union auditions are being done in your area. Then you click on the auditions that you think you are suitable for and you send the producers of that project your actor's headshot photo, resume and a link to your website so they can check out your performance video of your two contrasting scenes and your TV commercial. That's it.

If they like what they see they will contact you.

Do the seven steps as above, and you are now in the game!

You use this method to get as much non union work as you can to build up your actual work experience, build up the credits on your resume, collect your scenes from the project to upload on your website and hopefully replace the video you already have up there.

Finally, working on the non union projects gives you the opportunity to meet and network with other people in the same business as you, including the producers and the directors of those projects who may want to work with you again. It's up to you. One of my students got 15 independent films using this method and built up her resume and he experience and so can YOU!

Being An Extra / Getting Experience

Being an "extra" or "background" or "atmosphere" as the terms go is a great way to get in the door, make a few bucks, network and learn on the job. An extra is a person you might notice in the background of a scene; whose face you won't see but they might be just walking past or sitting reading with their back to the camera, etc.

MY PERSONAL MANAGER TIP: I would strongly suggest that new actors consider being an extra to get their foot in the door and learn on the job experiences at this early stage, without being the one who has to step into the limelight. You just want to learn the ropes, see how things work on a real production set and build your understanding of how it all works. It's a great place to begin.

Having "extra work" on your resume is not going to get you much work, but it's the knowledge you learn, and the experience you learn that is invaluable.

Just get in the door, and anything could happen. For example, the director might offer you a line to read in a scene, and suddenly, you have gone from being an extra to being a day-player.

You will also earn more money, and it's also a great start to your resume because you can put that "day-player" role as a credit on your resume.

Most cities have extras casting agencies. A lot of the time movies are being made where they will call on the extra agency to provide the "talent." They might want you to be on the set for an all-day shooting of scenes, and you get paid for it, or they might need you for just half a day. Check with the agents what the current pay-scale is for extras. Other options for you are any student films being produced at universities or performance schools or colleges.

Chapter Four

Also, you must try low budget, non-union productions or industrials. They are a great way to break into the business.

Many industrial video companies or corporate video training companies produce in-house sales training videos for business-to-business communications and corporate image dvds.

Also, post-production houses produce corporate videos and sales training videos. If you phone them, you can learn who casts for their videos and then when you are ready, get yourself out to that casting director for an initial meeting and or audition.

(Remember, always take a photo and resume with you, just in case the casting director asks for your photo or resume) AND REMEMBER TO HAVE TRAINING ON YOUR RESUME!!

Most times you will be asked for a photo and resume, or you will have to send in one of each, so be prepared. Get out to as many auditions as you can, even if you know you won't get the part. Reason being is, its experience, learn and sharpen your audition skills, plus, you get to meet up with the casting people and the director or producer, and get a chance to show them what you got.

You may not be the "right type" for the role you auditioned for. However, you may be right for something else that are doing. BUT- before you do this, make sure you know how to audition correctly.

You don't want to go into the audition room and make a complete fool of yourself. That would be a humiliating experience to say the least, also, the casting people may NEVER ask you back, and that may discourage you from doing future auditions. Don't blow your chances by being impatient and wanting it all NOW! So, take one step at a time.

First, get training and practice till you feel comfortable. If you are in a position to get a coach, that's all the better. Why struggle when you can access a professional coach who knows how to do it, because they have been there, and they know the pitfalls and advantages (from experience). They can coach you, and work on your audition skills, so when you walk into that audition, you will feel good about yourself and know that nothing can stop you. This may be all the edge you need to get that audition, so remember; if you can get a coach then do it.

Three of my students came to me one day and told me that they had to prepare for a performance school audition in a month.

They asked if I would do private coaching with them on their monologues. Well, we went to work on their monologues, and after six private sessions, they were ready. Meanwhile, another student asked me the day before her performance school audition if I would listen to her monologue and offer a few quick tips. "Yes," I said, and with that, the girl began her monologue. It was really terrible to sit through her performance. Oh my God! It was like pulling teeth. I mean, she was walking all over the stage, with no reason to do so. She was still struggling with her lines. She was speaking so fast, and her diction was awful, that I couldn't understand most of her words, because her pronunciations were so poor.

I asked her, why she didn't come to me a month ago for private classes, like the other three girls. She said that she didn't think about that; and that she thought _she could save money and do it herself._

Now think about this for a moment. Here is a simple case of four girls who know what they want, and they know they need coaching to help them get what they want, which is to get into a performance school of their dreams and begin building their careers. However, to get into the school, they needed private classes, and my classes cost them a total of $100.

Three of the four girls paid me the $100, and we worked hard, and they got into their dream schools, but the fourth girl messed up on her thinking and her timing. She thought she could do it herself, and save a few dollars. She also left her preparation until the last minute.

Chapter Four

Well, the four girls went into their auditions that week, along with over 700 others students, all auditioning for about 35 spaces in the schools and guess what? My three girls got in and the one who left everything to the last minute never made the cut.

That's a true story, check out the image on the next page.

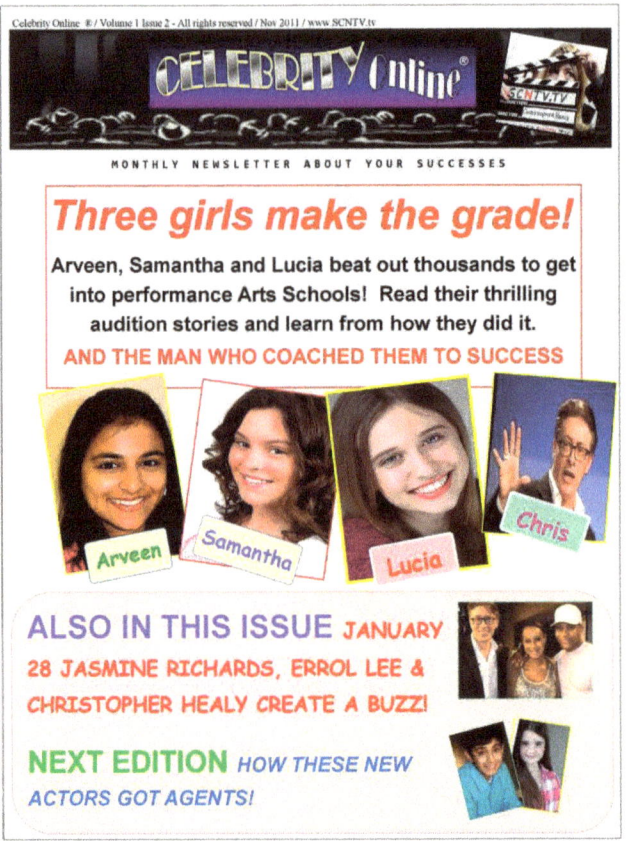

Remember to enter the audition room with a real smile and be professional.

MY PERSONAL MANAGER TIP: I strongly suggest that you do not think of the audition as an all or nothing fight to the death type of "test." This is a big mistake! Try thinking of your audition as a "performance"; a little performance but a performance none the less. This simple, yet powerful mental adjustment will shift everything to your advantage. You want to be a performer, don't you? Then go in and "perform" your heart out. In other words, don't see it as an all or nothing test, however, enjoy it immensely and you will be outstanding!

Marketing and Promotion

Agents, managers and casting people will usually go to local plays and community theatre to enjoy a good show, but also to see any young up and coming talent. That's why it's a good idea to do community theatre among other great reasons so that you can market yourself.

Get yourself into a local play and send out invitations with a 5 x 7 postcard picture of yourself with the name of the play, your address, and telephone number if you can drop in two complimentary tickets to sweeten the pot.

Send your postcard invites out to agents, managers, casting directors and producers. Send them out to whoever you can to get them to notice you.

If they are a casting director, write on your postcard that you would really like them to see your work. Let them know you are working in a play and that you would like for them to see your work. Provide them the details of the show, and when it's playing so, they have that option of coming to see you. If you only have a small role then hold off inviting them until you get a larger role.

Chapter Four

How To Use Social Media To Get More Acting Work

Whether you're looking to spread the word about your latest one-person show or get your face/name out there, the Internet is an essential tool for self-promotion. Social networking is a cheap alternative to print and commercial advertising, and user-generated content rules! Here are the big three websites with which to get familiar with.

1/ Facebook: Everyone uses Facebook, and for good reason, it's a vast networking landscape that you can access to your benefit. Facebook also has opportunities to create and advertise live events like plays, or whatever you are trying to promote. The event pages can be used by production companies as digital billboards for them to promote. If you are serious about acting then sign-up for free and create your own personal status updates and fan pages. If you have any plays or up-coming shows to promote then do it here. Invite your friends and their contacts to any shows or events that you are part of. It's time to begin getting seriously creative with your potential and get into self-promotion.

2/ Twitter: Twitter is all about what are you doing. Millions of people are twitting to let others know what's happening in their lives. It's a fabulous opportunity for you to use the 140 text characters allowed, to let others know what you're up to. You can also share photos with links, including videos and even audio. This means that you can update twitters with your acting headshots, or any self-tape auditions (be careful here and make sure that you do not upload anything before the production is released otherwise you could get into some serious copyright issues with the production companies). However, when your show does come out, you can release the trailer or whatever the event is. You can sign up to Twitter for free. You can also use Twitter across other social media platforms like Facebook, YouTube, MySpace, and dozens more.

3/ YouTube: Speaking of YouTube, you must know by now just how powerful this website has become. You sign up for free and upload your videos, and away you go. It's a great place to show what you can do, and so any prospecting agents or casting people can review your promo reel right there. I have many of my students use YouTube all the time, and then I call an agent to look at those students monologues. It works very well. Also, include in the description your name and any updates or link to your resume. It's a great tool to use

MY MANAGER TIP: Here is how to get you page noticed on Google and YouTube. Get YouTube viewers to subscribe to your channel. The more subscribers, the more your rankings improve. Also, if you have a blog or a website, make sure you embed your YouTube videos onto your blog and website. Next, add a new description for those videos on your blog or website, don't use the same description that you have on YouTube. Then for your "tag," add a link that leads back to your YouTube watch page for that video. Remember, when you are linking back, make sure that you use the heading or title that is on your YouTube video and use that heading as your "tag" highlighted link back to your YouTube video watch page.

Chapter Four

Personal Branding

We are all "brands," like it or not. If you are on the internet, then you are a brand. What is a personal brand? Personal branding is about people actively marketing themselves and their careers as "brands." Even if you are a school kid on the net, then you are already creating your brand for the entire world to see. So when people read about you or look at you, they are getting the concept of "who you are, and what you're about," and they're getting all that from your brand, your image – all connected to the internet.

There is a very real reality out there in the internet world, and it goes like this: you are what Google says you are. So control the message that others are reading about you. Build you as a "brand."

Also, a part of your brand is what people say about you online. If millions of people say your brand is crap and untrustworthy then your done, finished. If millions of people say you are amazing then millions more will buy into what you are offering.

So, learn to market yourself responsibly and wisely.

What is "marketing?" It's about sharing. Marketing is sharing, and today you have so many ways to get your brand out to the people. Start building your brand. Care about it, and cultivate it over the years. Remember, your personal brand is you, your personal life and your professional life. You want people to speak highly of you. You always want to make a good impression.

Here Is An Exercise For You

Write and memorize your own personal introduction. Pretend as if you are stepping up in front of a crowd, and you have 1 minute to use this introduction to show off your amazing personality. Tell them your name, who you are, and what you are about in an interesting and hopefully lighthearted way. Keep your introduction, upbeat, positive, and inspiring, but most of all, keep it genuine.

For example, tell us a little bit about you, your work, your personality, and your interests. Include any hobbies or anything unique. Remember, not to sway your body as you talk, keep your hands comfortably by your sides and NOT in your pockets or behind your back. Speak slowly and include your audience as in "talk to them" in conversation and not "talk at them." Talk to them like you are talking to your best friend.

Remember, that the majority of your impact will come from your tone of voice and body language. Communicate enthusiasm by smiling naturally and making direct eye contact.

Speak clearly with an upbeat, positive tone of voice and make it conversational. Also, try thinking about who are you introducing yourself to and why? What will they discover so interesting about you? What might you have in common with this person? What can you share with them that will quickly help you make a connection?

Oh, and if you are the type of person who speaks to fast, particularly when you are a little nervous meeting people, then try this exercise. Get a book and try reading out loud, one word at a time with a breath in between each work. So, take a little breath and then say the word, and take another little breath, and say the next word, and so on until the end of the page. Make sure you don't hyperventilate. Just take a natural breath after each word, and take your time as you follow this simple process to the end of the text.

Chapter Four

The more you practice this exercise, the more you will begin to slow down naturally.

In conclusion, your personal brand must be cultivated and developed over time. As your career moves along and evolves, keep updating it so people can follow along with the message you are painting for the world to see. And what's that message you are supposed to paint? That's up to you, but my advice is, keep it professional, even if you are a teenager, keep it clean. Keep it productive and upbeat, just like your upbeat personality.

Okay so now you know about your personal brand. You will need to represent yourself in a manner that's similar to your brand. This means that you need to put so thought into what your 'brand" is and how do you want to be seen. Think about that.

MY MANAGER TIP: Think as If, you were invited to speak about yourself on the Larry King show for five minutes, what would you say about yourself? How would you dress? How would you be seen, seated, hunched over or sitting up, looking stiff and awkward or relaxed? Would you want to be seen NOT knowing what to do with your hands? Would you be seen biting your nails or would you want to be seen smiling, breathing and listening to your host? How would you want the viewers to see you? What impression would you want them to have of you? That's your brand. Build it, own it and look after it. Your brand is your reputation. For actors, think "leading man or Leading woman."

Below I have included some personal branding tips for you to consider and remember:

- People want to know they can trust you so be trustworthy
- Education/training is important, however, what matters most is the application and presentation of your knowledge
- Hone your listening skills. Most people don't listen. They think they do, but they don't

- Take your shyness into the backyard and bury it forever. Stop playing the "I'm shy" stuff because it's what will get you nowhere fast
- Making first AND last impressions are super important. So, how you enter, and how you leave them wanting more is important. And remember, to show your best at all times, especially before, during and after rough moments
- Find ways to make your own mark in whatever it is you are thinking. Make it yours. Own it. Consider standing out rather than blending in. And remember to be yourself and not the latest trend
- Be an entrepreneur. Think like an entrepreneur. Behave like an entrepreneur
- You want to be openly loyal to your family. You want to be around people who respect this quality. We are judged heavily by our relationship with our family
- Get in shape. Work that body and think like a leading player
- Bad breath can ruin the atmosphere, and bad body odor is the worst! Take a shower each day, and don't overdo it on the "hide the odor" sports sprays
- Be magnetic. Be truthful. Be playful. Be powerful
- Demonstrate your knowledge and understanding of your industry by creating relevant content (blog posts, videos, images, etc.)

Chapter Four

Your 10 Step Show Business Plan To Acting Success

FIRST UP, YOU MUST PLAN YOUR WORK

Step /1: Learn everything you can about the acting industry

Step /2: Get acting training. Get physically fit. Get confidence

Step /3: Get your headshots

Step /4: Prepare your Resume and Cover Letter

Step /5: Get an "extras" agent to get real "on set" experience

Step /6: Find acting work by signing onto casting websites

Step /7: Get Non union acting work to build experience

Step /8: If possible, get a demo reel together

Step /9: Get a principal agent and aim for the union work

Step /10: Audition, network, learn, and strive to succeed and always be professional

Those ten steps above can take at least two years to complete, and possibly more. Are you really ready to take on that responsibility? Are you hungry enough? Then go for it with all the passion you can muster, and you might just do it.

Now that you have your plan, the final thing to do is work your plan to success!

Success Strategies For Monologues

When doing a scene or monologue, remember to ask yourself the following questions:

1 / Who are you?

2 / Where are you?

3 / Where are you in the story of the play or movie?

4 / Who are you talking to?

5 / What do you want from them? (That's your objective)

6 / What tactics are you going to use during the course of the monologue to get what you want?

7 / How is the person you're talking to responding to what you're saying?

Understand the background of the monologue; you do this by reading the entire play.

Seriously consider calling in a professional acting coach, they can help develop your monologue or scene into a professional punch that may get you the job.

Don't just pick any old monologue. It's important that you pick a monologue that connects to you in a personal way. Pick something that you like.

Don't try to learn a monologue in two days. Be smart and give yourself time to fully prepare and relax into the role. It's important you use variety in your pitch, variety in your volume, and variety in the rhythm. Make sure you understand every word and ENUNCIATE clearly.

Chapter Four

Whatever the scene or commercial is, it's important that you know your gestures and their places in advance. You must love the work you do.

Auditioning Tips

• Always be on time and NEVER be late.

• Always take headshots and resumes with you into all auditions.

• Enter the audition room smiling, upbeat and relaxed.

• Make sure you stand on your mark.

• Listen, listen, listen, to what you are being told.

• Don't say your monologue to them; pick a spot over their heads or between their heads.

• Don't bring props.

• Focus, focus, focus, on what you are doing.

• When you are in the audition, NEVER RUSH you work, instead, breathe and take your time.

• Try not to use swear words.

• Make sure that one of your monologue pieces is comedic.

• Don't move unnecessarily on the stage or around your mark. Be an actor who is grounded in stillness, that's more effective than movement just for movement's sake. Only move when you have a reason to move.

• Never hold your breath, always remember to breathe.

• Remember personalize the camera by talking to your best friend.

- Relax, breathe, know your lines, believe in yourself and have fun.

- Make the audition your own by adding your qualities to it.

- When the off camera actor is saying his lines make sure you are watching him and listening to what he says. Don't be reading your lines as he speaks. Keep your eyes up.

- Listen and react authentically.

Chapter Four

Tips For Comedy

1 / Add character flaws that can add humor.

2 / Repeat something three times and on the last time add a twist.

3 / The "set-up" and the "Punch line" means make every joke and every comedy story made of this

4 / Vulnerability can be very funny. Learn how to play it up.

5 / Timing: This is the rhythm of the scene and also comedic pauses which have to be not too long or too short, and at the right moment.

6/ Miscommunication is funny when people miss understand, and this can be played up into humorous situations. Example is Abbott and Costello's 'who's on First" on YouTube. I have used this skit many times with my students over the years.

Film, Television, Acting Definitions

These definitions will help you out so learn them well.

• Screenplay: is the script written for a film.

• Production Company: is the company with the resources to bring the screenplay to life and the film to market.

• Pre-production: is the period before filming begins when special tasks are to be completed, such as the selection of actors for the various roles in the film.

• Post-production: is the period after filming ends when scenes are edited.

• SAG: short for Screen Actors Guild. SAG is the largest film union

• SAG eligible: when an actor becomes SAG eligible, it means he or she has met the requirements needed to enter the Screen Actors Guild. That is, they have either performed one principal role in a union film or have met some other SAG requirement for entry.

• Crew: Crew, in film, refers to the team hired by a production company to assist in the production of the film.

• Production assistant: is the main person who assists the producer on a set.

• Assistant director: is the person who assists the director ion the set.

• Film extra: an extra is an actor/performer whose main role in the film is to provide background scenery to create the illusion of reality.

• Trailer: A trailer is a collection of clips, usually from an upcoming film, used to generate an interest in the film.

• Action: When the director of a film calls out "Action!" it is the verbal cue for the actors to begin the performance.

• Cut: When the director calls out "cut," the scene has ended. Stay where you are until directed what to do next.

• Frame: Frame refers to the area of focus of the camera's lens without the camera moving.

• Industrial: is a film that is used for private corporate marketing or educational purposes.

• Off-camera: when an actor is said to be off-camera, it simply means that that actor is out of the camera's view.

• Set: Set refers to the area where the performance of the scenes takes place.

Chapter Four

• Clapper Board or Slate: The device used in a film to identify the various takes in the film, as in "Take 1".

• Take: A take is a segment in which a scene is performed, as in "Take 1!".

• It's a Wrap: is a verbal command used by the director to signify the end of the day's shooting. "That's a wrap."

• Call time: is the time that the actor or model is to have arrived and be prepared for work.

• Casting: refers to the process of selecting an actor for a particular role or assignment.

• Casting Notice: refers to the list of characteristics the actor should likely have to fulfill the role.

• Day rate: refers to the about of money the actor receives for a day of work.

• Demo Reel: refers to a video or DVD containing samples of work the actor has performed captured on film.

• Principle or Lead is the person in a commercial or show who dominates the action.

• Props: are the articles that are used to assist in the role or action, such as chairs, cups, balls and virtually any object on the set.

• Residual: is the money paid to the actor each time their commercial is run unless there is a separate agreement not to issue residuals.

• AFTRA: Is the largest union for television, commercial and radio actors. It stands for the American Federation of Television and Radio Artists.

• Teleprompter: is a monitor that scrolls down the actor's lines as the actor is performing. This is similar to the monitors used by news and anchor people. It helps actors with their lines.

• Outtakes: are the scenes which are taken out in the final editing process.

• Pan refers to the horizontal shift of the camera from left to right, as in "pan to the left."

Suggested Reading

- Approach to Acting by Sanford Meisner
- Acting for the Camera by Tony Barr
- Acting for the camera by Michael Cain
- An Actor prepares by Constantine Stanislavski
- A Challenge for the Actor by Uta Hagen
- Audition by Michael Shurtleff
- Actors Survival kit by Miriam Newhouse & Peter Messaline CANADA
- Getting Organized from Theatre Ontaion.org and also get the Agents Book
- The Actors Survival Guide by Jon Robbins USA
- Actors Working by Clair Sinnett – USA Casting Director
- Meisner for Teens by Larry Silverberg
- Larry Silverberg: The Sanford Meisner Approach: An Actor's Workbook – Book 1 through 4
- Life Lessons From An Acting Class
- What's So Special About You?
- What's So Special About US?

What's So Special About YOU?

I strongly suggest that you read my book, ***What's So Special About YOU?*** Everyone wishes for happiness and success, but most of us spend our days locked in survival mode because we don't believe that our dreams can come true. We're just not special enough. On a deeper level, we are too afraid to believe in our true potential. We hide behind distractions or excuses and live second-rate lives as "nothing special," yet deep inside us burns a profound desire to be more of who we truly are.

"What's So Special About YOU?" compiles and presents a surprisingly fresh perspective revealed through 77 winning qualities, strategies, and principles used consistently by the world's most successful people, that transforms lives from ordinary to extraordinary. Now, this empowering knowledge is available for you to cultivate the richness and happiness you deserve.

BOOK REVIEWS:

"Christopher Healy brilliantly weaves two separate narratives into one book. WHAT'S SO SPECIAL ABOUT YOU? asks the reader to discover and analyze their 'true self,' by applying 77 winning principles as a life-changing tool to compile a composite score of their 'best self,' while following a compelling nine-week odyssey of twelve young people who made the same discovery in an interactive class setting." **Andrew Terry Pasieka, Editor-in-Chief, SMJ Magazine**

"***Authentic, Authoritative, Awesome.*** *Christopher Healy takes the perennial personal success formula and does what is incredibly unique for this mature genre...he actually put in practice and documents the progress of a group of his students through their own reflections. This is framed within a structured class style curriculum with material that is well referenced. Enlightening and uplifting - Mr. Healy's narrative and direction reads easily, and every paragraph has something to offer with nods given, where appropriate to the greats of the success mentoring industry.*

The target audience is wide and the content applicable to the entertainment, entrepreneurial and professional markets. A sales team that has gone through this course would be formidable indeed. The book is that good." **Steve Perpich - Management Consultant - New York City Event Insider.**

"*Healy's book is deep, sustained, timely and highly relevant. His book is well researched based on proven case studies of its life-changing nature. His book provides a welcome, new synthesis of practical and professional knowledge and experience which is* **Groundbreaking in its impact.** *Healy is on the verge of creating a new field of study and practice in which the thespian capabilities are put in the service of persons who not only wish to be successful actors but who may wish to experience a broader life success overall."* **H.T. Wilson former Professor of Law and Business Management.**

WHAT'S IN THE BOOK!

- 77 qualities, strategies and principles from the world's most successful people to help change your life
- Real life (adversity to success) students first-person accounts and inspirational real-life examples
- Take the "ten-rounds" of success by design challenges and see how you rate with the world's best
- Lifting yourself from feeling "self-defeated" to being fully empowered
- Fantastic stories of success from people who were less than successful, to inspire you on your journey

So, open the book on the 77 life-changing qualities of the world's most successful people, and learn why they are so successful at being so successful. Then take the self-assessment success challenge within and see how you rate with the best because now is the time to discover what's so special about YOU!

Visit: **www.SpecialYouInsider.com**

The Actors Success In The Making

Check Out The Classes

Christopher Healy Coaching
Performance & Creative Leadership — **Skills for Life!**

UNIQUE CLASSES FOR KIDS & TEENS IN THORNHILL
Professional Acting on Camera / TV Commercials / Film /
Stagecraft / Monologues / Showcases / Nurturing Confidence
Auditions & Media interviews / Business Acumen / Team dynamics
Creative Leadership & High Performance thinking!

CELEBRATING 20+YEARS TEACHING & COACHING!
Clients include...

Rachel Parent
ENVIRONMENTAL
WORLDWIDE
SENSATION!

Jordan Clark
TV Star
The Next Step!

William Healy
Stars as Cartoon
Voices of
Franklin
& Arthur!

Ana Golja
TV STAR
DEGRASSI
Next generation

Brianna Ramagnano
Stars in
Paranormal Witness
& Web of Lies!

Congratulations to Karol!
For being accepted in
Cardinal Carter Academy!
"Karol is the happiest kid in the
world. Thank you for preparing
him" – His Dad

SHE DOES IT AGAIN!
Qadira gets **TV commercial for
PRIME MEATS** and TV show
EARTH RANGERS!

FIRST SHE LANDS THE AGENT THEN
10 year old Romy lands TV SPOT FOR
BOSTON PIZZA and TV SERIES -
FEAR THY NEIGHBOUR!

"It's much more than acting; it's self confidence and life skills building, which every child needs" - Sharon Ramagnano parent of student.

Visit www.**ChristopherHealy.ca**

The Actors Success In The Making

REVIEWS ABOUT HIS TEACHING:

Christopher Healy's classes are described by students and parents as **"Phenomenal! Exceptional! Life-changing!**

"Christopher Healy has a teaching style as powerful as that of Tony Robbins. He reaches deep into the psyche of unreachable teenagers, and I spires them to be the best they can be!"– Rebecca DiFilppo Publisher of Moods magazine

"Chris is a natural teacher!" Clair Sinnett -Hollywood Casting Director

"Chris is amazing!" As seen on Breakfast Television

I truly hope you were able to gain insightful knowledge, clarity, and inspiration to move yourself forward in the right direction. Just remember to live life fearlessly, stay healthy and live free.

You can always visit me at www.ChristopherHealy.ca

Thank you for hanging in there with me.

Good luck and enjoy the journey of living your dreams.

Chris.

The End.

The Actors Success In The Making

www.ingramcontent.com/pod-product-compliance
Lightning Source LLC
Chambersburg PA
CBHW040328300426
44113CB00020B/2692